Peace
WITHIN
YOUR BORDERS

DEVOTIONS
FOR HOME
SCHOOL
TEACHERS

BETH SHARPTON

Peace Within Your Borders

. . . .

Published by WinePress Publishing
PO Box 428 Enumclaw, WA 98022.

•

•

All Scripture quotations, unless otherwise noted, are taken from the
HOLY BIBLE, NEW INTERNATIONAL VERSION.
Copyright © 1973, 1978, 1984 International Bible Society.
Used by permission of Zondervan Bible Publishers.

•

All definitions in this work are taken from
The Second College Edition of The American Heritage Dictionary
(Boston: Houghton Mifflin Company, 1982, 1985).

•

ISBN 1-57921-219-0
Library of Congress Catalog Card Number: 99-60965

Cover & interior design by: DesignPoint, Inc., Salem, OR

Dedicated

to Jeff, whose love and

encouragement have stretched

and comforted me along the way.

And to Tara and Launa, whose

antics fill my days with delight and

force me to my knees for

guidance and wisdom.

Table of Contents

Warm-up Bonus:
Dressed for Success   1

September: *Gearing Up*
    1. Let's Acknowledge God   4
    2. Stirred Up and Sent Out   8
    3. Why Am I Doing This?   12
    4. A Hopeful Outlook   16

October: *Modeling*
    1. Aspire to be Worthy   20
    2. Hear Big   24
    3. Do You Love Me?   28
    4. Soaking Up His Scent   32

November: *Giving Thanks*
    1. Your Love is Ever Before Me   36
    2. Joy-filled Thanks   40
    3. A Reason to Sing   44
    4. Shouting With Joy   48

December: *Praising God*
    1. All for the Glory of God   52
    2. Excel in Giving   56
    3. Shining Ever Brighter   60
    4. Why I Teach   64

January: *The Winter Freeze*
1. Daily — 68
2. Energizing Power — 72
3. Stones of Remembrance — 76
4. Peace Within Your Borders — 80

February: *What I Need to Be*
1. He Cares for the Caregiver — 84
2. His Wisdom; His Strength — 88
3. Darkness is Passing — 92
4. Velvet Covered Steel — 96

March: *There are Rewards*
1. Resting in Victory — 100
2. Not Worthy to be Compared — 104
3. The Skilled Worker — 108
4. Needing Affirmation — 112

April: *Planting for a Future Harvest*
1. What Kind of Smart Are You? — 116
2. Second Chances — 120
3. Following at a Distance — 124
4. Pleasant Words — 128

May: *Sending Them Forth*
1. Giving Lavish Praise — 132
2. Speaking of God… — 136
3. Tell…Proclaim! — 140
4. Passing on the Faith — 144

End-of-the-Year Bonus:
Waiting for the Harvest — 148

Foreword

Beth knowingly goes right to the heart of a home educating mom. It's too easy to begin the day by leaping to the attention of the thousands of things that beckon us. Everything around us tries to tear down the godly families for which our hearts hunger. Where is the peace the Lord our God promises? Beth's precious words and insights remind us that it is delightful to have friends who share many of the same struggles that we do and can give us encouragement and focus at the moment we need it. Her words are those of a dear friend with insight that renews and refreshes.

Anxiety in a man's heart weighs him down (Proverbs 12:25). God is there, however, waiting for us to let go of the weight and receive His peace and be glad in the work He has given us to do. Beth gently but firmly pulls us – mothers who take seriously and personally the education of our children – back to this truth and assurance.

Betsy and Dr. Brian Ray

Betsy Ray is a home schooling mother of eight children who have all always been home educated. Dr. Brian Ray is the internationally known researcher and president of the National Home Education Research Institute (NHERI). You can learn more about facts and statistics on home schooling and its successes by contacting NHERI at (503) 364-1490.

Preface

Thank you for taking the time to read this before you begin *Peace Within Your Borders*. My prayer is that you will experience peace this year in your home and school. I know that, like me, you will have days when the walls close in on you.

I have written this book of devotions so you would not feel alone, so you would know there are others who face the same dilemmas you do. The joys and sorrows of a home schooler are somewhat different from those of other parents. I felt the need for a book of devotions specifically for our needs. We are on the road together, so let us lift each other up and be encouraged by the Lord.

I love the words of 2 Corinthians 1:3-4, "Praise be to the God and Father of our Lord Jesus Christ, the Father of compassion and the God of all comfort, who comforts us in all our troubles, so that we can comfort those in any trouble with the comfort we ourselves have received from God."

Each week, whether you read on Monday morning before the onslaught of the week, or on the weekend between the past and future, I hope you will sit down with a cup of coffee, or curled up in your favorite spot, and revel in His Word for you.

Love in Christ,
Beth Sharpton

WARM-UP BONUS

Dressed FOR SUCCESS

She is clothed with strength and dignity;
she can laugh at the days to come.
She speaks with wisdom,
and faithful instruction is on her tongue.
Proverbs 31:25-26

Some days it's fun to dress up a little and wear "teacher" clothes, especially on field trip days. But since I walk the dog at recess in all weather, my "dress for success" outfit doesn't consist of a gray power-suit and pumps, but t-shirt and jeans, or casual pants. I try to look clean and neat, having hair and makeup done before we begin our school day, but there are those days when I hope and pray the FedEx man doesn't come to the door.

Even on those days when my outward appearance isn't all I'd like it to be, I strive to keep my inward self dressed and ready. King Lemuel expounded on the qualities of a noble woman in Proverbs 31. Included in that is a dress code: "she is clothed in strength and dignity."

A noble woman commands respect from her children and others around her, not because she demands it, but because of who she is in the Lord. This is not a grab and go outfit. The noble woman takes time and care to clothe herself in this ensemble, listening to God and responding in obedience.

Other "dress for success" verses list these items of apparel: compassion, kindness, humility, gentleness, patience, salvation, righteousness, power, and Christ himself (Job 29:14; Is. 61:10; Luke 24:49; Rom. 13:14; Gal. 3:27; Col. 3:12; 1 Pet. 5:5).

What better place for a teacher to go shopping for school clothes than to bow at the throne of Jesus? This is the best preparation we can make for the coming school year. The price tag is time, humility, and a sincere and listening heart. But these are garments worth the price; they never wear out and they're always in style!

Dear Lord, I want to get ready for this school year by concentrating on what's most important. I do care about my outward appearance. I am your temple bearing witness to you, and how I treat this body teaches my children habits for a healthy lifestyle. But more than anything, I want to be clothed with your character. Cover me today, dear Jesus; cover my nakedness with your holiness, your love, your patience, your very self. Amen.

September

GEARING UP

Let's
ACKNOWLEDGE GOD

Let us acknowledge the LORD;
let us press on to acknowledge him.
As surely as the sun rises,
he will appear;
he will come to us like the winter rains,
like the spring rains that water the earth.

Hosea 6:3

*T*his was our theme verse for the year. I wrote it in large letters on posterboard and surrounded the words with pictures of rich, vibrant flowers and posted it above my desk in the schoolroom. Some days we read it together, but most of the time it was a reminder for me — my goal for the year. Even though our theme changes from year to year, I don't want to forget what I learned from this verse.

Every day in some way, I want to acknowledge God — not just in our morning prayer, like a nod as we pass on the street. I want to welcome Him as our special invited Guest, Principal of the school, Friend of every student and teacher, Leader and Guide, Counselor, and Originator of all knowledge.

It takes effort. We must press on to acknowledge Him, for sometimes He gets forgotten as the day wears long and we grow weary. Emotions roller coaster and we tire of the constant rubbing of personalities. We have to stop and look at Him again to receive instructions, forgiveness, blessings.

That's when we truly see Him — when we look. Of course, we know He will one day appear in all His glory and we will see Him as He is. But even now, We can realize He is here just as surely as the sun rises each morning.

God's faithfulness is like the winter and spring rains. Living in Salem, Oregon, we know more of the faithfulness of rain than of the rising sun, which we sometimes doubt is even there beyond the clouds. The rain here is faithful. Hosea says God will come like that, if we train ourselves to notice—cool and refreshing rain, nourishing, cleansing, bringing color and new growth.

God will rain down on us to feed our thirsty souls.

Holy God, how I long to
make this verse my own.
Help me acknowledge you
each day with reverence
and grateful praise, and to
expect you to come as
much as I expect the sun
to rise and the rain to fall.
May my children learn
this kind of expectancy
from my example. May
they learn to recognize
your presence in their inner
being. We acknowledge you
Lord, and our deep need for
you. You are wonderful
beyond compare. We praise
you! We welcome you into
our classroom this week,
Lord. Amen.

Stirred
UP AND SENT OUT

Like an eagle that stirs up its nest
and hovers over its young,
that spreads its wings to catch them
and carries them on its pinions.
Deuteronomy 32:11

Eagles are known for their majestic beauty, their skill in hunting, for the pride they bring to the American heart. Not many would think to praise them for their skill as parents. Yet several times in the Bible God is likened to an eagle in the way He cares for His people.

These verses in Deuteronomy refer to the stirring of the nest—when the parent eagle nudges, even pushes the eaglets out of the nest to try their wings. But they are not left to their own devices. The parent hovers over the young, always close by in case there's trouble. And when they make their fledgling flight the eagles watch with a keen eye. If anything goes awry, they will catch the eaglet on their back and return it to the safety of the nest.

God does that for us. He challenges us into flight, then hovers over to see how we're doing. And if we begin to fall, for whatever reason, He comes beneath to catch us on His mighty wings. He carries us to safety in the strength of His mighty power.

God said to the Israelites, "I carried you on eagles' wings and brought you to myself" (Exodus 19:4). He did not bring them out of Egypt just to make a new "nest" for them in the

Promised Land. He brought them out so they might know Him. And that's what He longs to do for us today. He wants us to fly in faith and allow Him to be our comfort and security.

Have you been afraid to leave the safety of your nest and fly out on faith? Are you thinking about home schooling, but haven't made the leap yet because of fear? Or do you need to make a change in what you're doing in your school, family life, relationships, or church ministry? If you feel stirred up inside and have no peace about where you are now, perhaps God is preparing you to leave the nest.

Or perhaps you've had a flight failure lately: a child rebelling against your authority, a lack of progress in a certain subject. Has your own anger led you to say words you now regret? Rest on the wings that have come to rescue you. If you do, He will bring you into His Holy presence where there is healing and strength.

Oh Father, I don't really
want to leave the nest, it's
so warm and safe here,
but if there is any area of
my life you are stirring
me to step out and take
flight in, help me to obey.
I'm glad you care enough
to make sure I land all
right. I need the assurance
that you won't let me fall.
If I didn't know your
wings were beneath to
catch me when I fall,
I would never have the
courage to try. Thank you
for being there, drawing
me closer to you. I love
you, Lord. Amen.

Why
AM I DOING THIS?

So that your trust may be in the LORD,
I teach you today, even you.
Proverbs 22:19

$\mathcal{O}$ne day as we were driving by the grade school our then six-year-old Launa asked, "Why do we home school?" She wanted to know why she didn't get to go to the public school her sister, Tara, had attended her first grade year. She was enticed by thoughts of making friends with the hundreds of other children there and a chance to ride the yellow school bus that passes our house everyday.

I answered by explaining it was a decision Daddy and I had made when Tara asked us to home school her. It had taken a lot of prayer, and we asked a lot of questions of God and others before we began.

Everything I said was true, but it sounded weak, even to me, because at the time I was struggling with the same question myself. Tara had *asked* to be home schooled, but Launa longed for the fun and excitement of going to school. As she and I clashed repeatedly, I began to wonder if perhaps she would be better off with another teacher. Again, I prayed for direction.

God answered my questions in a most unexpected way. He gave me the answer I needed through a National Geographic special on kangaroos.

The central story was of two mothers and their joeys. Eucalypt was an excellent mother, attentive to her daughter Sunshade's needs. Eucalypt taught her carefully about her environment and responded to her pleas for help and reassurance. She occasionally ran practice drills, barking the command for Sunshade to jump into the safety of her pouch.

The narrator had also introduced us to

Columbine and her son, Jaffa. Columbine was more interested in feeding herself than answering Jaffa's calls when he wandered too far away. Jaffa had trouble finding his mother's pouch at all and received no help from Columbine in his bungling attempts to reach the security he needed. He was smaller than Eucalypt's baby, Sunshade, although they were the same age, but he seemed full of curiosity and vigor. Perhaps everything would turn out all right.

But one day the mob was disturbed from their resting place by a rustling in the bush and Jaffa was separated from his mother. Young roos are taught to hide in the grass when this happens and wait for their mother to come back for them, but Jaffa was impatient and wandered far from where they had been.

The dingos went hunting that night. One joey was killed and its mother wounded. Jaffa's mother found him in the morning mangled and bleeding, having somehow escaped the wild dogs. He used the last of his strength to follow Columbine to a place of safety, but there was nothing she could do except watch over Jaffa as he lay dying. The narrator said her mournful cries were heard for two days. All of Columbine's eight joeys had died. Eucalypt, on the other hand, had successfully reared several joeys who were all healthy members of the kangaroo mob.

Now I know what to answer when our girls (or I) ask why we home school. I was like Columbine, going my own way, intent on feeding myself. I loved my children, but was not always swift to answer their cries. But now I realize it's my job to teach them how to feed on God's Word and what would be dangerous for them to consume. We also have "practice drills" (prayer) when problems arise, so our children will know where to run for safety when the enemy lurks nearby.

Jeff and I rejoice to see them becoming grounded in the faith—secure in a happy (if not always clean) home, able to reach out to others with compassion, pursuing answers to their doubts and concerns in an atmosphere of truth.

I have to admit there are days when I'd rather go shopping, pursue my own career, get the house clean, or quietly escape to a corner to read instead of spending my time teaching, correcting, inspiring, rebuking, and grading papers. But when Satan comes seeking whom he may devour, I pray our children will run to the Fortress of safety and escape the fate of so many children in our world today, who wander wounded and afraid.

Oh my God, my Rock and my Deliverer. Thank you for being our sure defense. Help me today to resolve to teach my children so that their trust may be in you. More than anything, I pray that they will grow to love you supremely, and be able to give a reason for the hope they have. And may we, together, reach out to those who have no hope and tell them how much you love them. Amen.

A
HOPEFUL OUTLOOK

I have great confidence in you;
I take great pride in you.
I am greatly encouraged;
in all our troubles my joy knows no bounds.

2 Corinthians 7:4

*C*arol began the Parenting Workshop by reading a verse she had printed on a huge pad of white paper, 2 Corinthians 7:4. She talked briefly about how she and her husband attempt to communicate these thoughts to their children in their words and actions everyday. She went on to say many other valuable things, but time after time my attention was pulled back to the verse in front of us. The words beckoned like a siren's sweet song. I knew this message was for me.

This is what my children need to hear from me—a message of hope and cheer:

> *that I have confidence in them, that we are proud of them, encouraged by their progress and full of joy, even when we go through troubled times as a family.*

Too often I forget to give my children these words of praise. I'm more zeroed in on what needs improvement, what they missed on the last test. I'm so busy weeding out those nasty attitudes that tend to creep in. I forget to tell them how pleased I am with what they're doing right.

There were many problems in the Corinthian church that the Apostle Paul had to address in his letters to the believers—divisions in the church, immorality, lawsuits, misuse of spiritual freedom and spiritual gifts, and more—

but he never failed to encourage them as well with heartening words of love. They could not doubt his devotion to them and his concern for their welfare.

As the month of September draws to a close, there may be some areas that are not going so well with one or all of your children. Pray for wisdom and strength and patience as you handle these difficulties, but also look for ways to tell each child that you have confidence in him — you're proud of him; you're encouraged with his progress; you rejoice he was born, even if you are now in the midst of troubles.

We'll be doing the same at our house.

Dear God, sometimes as a parent/teacher I get so focused on marking what is wrong that I forget to remark on what is right. Help me to look past the little problems of today and into the future, with hope. Let me pass along words of blessing to our precious children this week. In your Name, Amen.

October

MODELING

Aspire
TO BE WORTHY

Some faced jeers and flogging, while still others were chained and put in prison. They were stoned; they were sawed in two; they were put to death by the sword. They went about in sheepskins and goatskins, destitute, persecuted and mistreated — the world was not worthy of them.
Hebrews 11:36-38a

The girls and I had already waded through aisle after aisle of black and orange, with goblins and ghosts peeking at us around every bend. But when we got to the cash register it was our turn. The cashier looked at my two beautiful blonde-haired girls and asked the inevitable, "So, are you girls ready for Halloween?"

Tara, the older of the two, answered with enthusiasm, "Oh, we don't celebrate Halloween. We celebrate the Christian holiday of All Saints Day on November 1. We have a feast and play games and decorate the house and everything!"

We suddenly had the full attention of two cashiers and the woman bagging our groceries. They had many questions and the girls and I answered happily. Before we left the grocery store that day we had made new friends and witnessed rays of God's light shining into the dark month of October.

I sometimes dread October with its skeletons and demon-faced apparitions in stores and every catalog that enters our home, as America gears up for Halloween. But we've begun to look forward to those unsuspecting questioners, because it gives us a wonderful opportunity to tell others about an alternative.

All Saints Day, celebrated on November 1 was originally added to the Christian calendar to offset the wild pagan rituals associated with harvest and fertility in the fall. It was a day set aside to honor all those martyred for Christ. It wasn't long before superstitious beliefs muddied people's understanding of the celebration. People began to believe that on (Halloween) the eve of All Saints Day, (also called All Hallows), evil spirits were allowed to walk the earth, playing tricks on people. And so began the practices of setting out treats to appease the spirits, and dressing as demons, so as not to be recognized if one had to be out on business (or to collect treats). Unfortunately, the eve of the holiday (holy day) became more popular than the holiday itself, as Christians were drawn into the new pagan celebrations. When we learned this, we decided it was time to reclaim the day for holy partying.

Now we spend the month of October reading Christian biographies. We sing hymns and contemporary songs that rejoice in faith and courage. We decorate the house with red and white banners (the colors of courage and faith), and invite others to join us for a feast on All Saints Day to remember all Christians who have gone before us. And we play our own game of "Who's Who in Christian history?"

Why not dedicate the month of October to learning about our inspiring heritage instead of being inundated by fear and darkness? Early Christians who were martyred for the sake of the Name, monks who kept faith alive through the Dark Ages, the participants in the Reformation, missionaries, pioneers, and modern day heroes—all these famous and obscure people carried the torch to the next generation so we might know Christ's love. I am only beginning to learn. How I wish I'd started earlier!

Dear God, encourage each member of our family to exemplify a faith that can't be watered down. Help us to draw strength from our heritage. I admit I fear having to face even a small amount of persecution. Christians have endured, and continue to suffer a tremendous amount of pain, because they were willing to stand on your side no matter what the cost. Help me to be worthy to bear your Name in this world today. We aspire to be men and women of faith. Amen.

Hear
BIG

"If anyone has ears to hear, let him hear."
"Consider carefully what you hear," he continued.
"With the measure you use, it will be measured
to you—and even more."
Mark 4:23-24

I don't always hear well, even though I have the right appendages attached to my head. Just recently our home school group traveled to Portland to see the play, *The Wind in the Willows*. Everyone met at our house to carpool, except one mom, Crystal. She was running her two youngest children to a sitter at the far end of town. Three of us met and waited for the fourth mom, Martha, and her kids to come, but when they didn't arrive we assumed they were with Crystal.

On the way to Portland I began to panic. Had we left Martha behind without directions or a note of where we were going? I felt like a rotten friend.

I was so relieved when we got there and Martha was indeed with Crystal. "I told you she was coming with me," Crystal looked at me curiously. She recounted our telephone conversation from that morning to me, but it didn't sound familiar. My ears had been there on the side of my head the whole time, but apparently I had been too distracted by my own thoughts for them to work properly.

Sometimes that happens when God is talking to me as well. I want to have ears to hear when He speaks, so I don't panic on the road thinking I've left behind something terribly important. But hearing the message is only part of it.

Jesus also said to consider what we hear. It's not enough to receive the message; I need to process that message and realize His plan for me. This takes time spent in reading and prayer and seeking His face. Then comes the final step. I need to act on what I'm hearing.

Whatever measure I use, God will use in giving back to me. I don't think Jesus was talking about giving material things only, but every part of our selves to Him. He will speak to us in proportion to the measure in which we hear. Why else would these verses run into each other the way they do?

Jesus said, give big, God will be generous with you. Hear big, God will load up your ears with more of His words of love and instruction and wisdom. If we embrace His truth, make it part of our lives, God will speak to us again and again. But if we don't receive what He says it would be useless for Him to keep sending us messages.

Doesn't this work with our children and in all of our relationships as well? When we hear what they are saying to us, either in the words they speak or by their manner, aren't we rewarded by knowing them in a fuller measure? But if we shut them out and their words fall to the ground, there will be fewer and fewer attempts made by them to be heard by us.

Three important things to remember about hearing:

1. If anyone has ears to hear, let him hear
2. Consider carefully what you hear
3. With the measure you use, it will be measured to you

Lord, I want to hear your voice. Don't let me miss it because my thoughts are elsewhere. I want to hear BIG. And with my children, Lord, help me listen to their words and even to their unspoken messages. Oh, how easy it is to tune them out sometimes, especially after we have interacted so closely all day in school. Help me to have ears to hear what's important. Amen.

Do YOU LOVE ME?

Jesus said, "Do you truly love me more than these?"
"Yes, Lord you know that I love you."
Jesus said, "Feed my lambs."
Again Jesus said, "Do you truly love me?"
"Yes, Lord, you know that I love you."
Jesus said, "Take care of my sheep."
A third time he said, "Do you love me?"
"Lord, you know all things, you know that I love you."
Jesus said, "Feed my sheep."
Then he said to him, "Follow me!"
taken from John 21:15-19

First, Jesus asked Peter whether he loved Him "more than these." He could have meant "more than you love these men," or "more than these men love me," or "more than you love these boats and nets." I must ask myself these same questions: Do I love Him more than I love any other person in the world? Have I boasted (either out loud or in my own heart) of having a greater commitment to Him than others do and then denied Him? Do I love Him more than what is familiar and comfortable and secure?

I've heard many sermons on the three "Do you love me's," expounding on the different meaning in the Greek for the word "love" each time, but never on the three different descriptions of the flock to which Jesus referred. But I found a lesson in the wording there for me as a Christian home schooler.

First of all Jesus said, "feed my lambs." To me that means I need to nourish not only my own little lambs on the milk of His Word (which is why most of us are home schooling in the first place), but all lambs that come within my reach, for they are all His. This means I need to use every opportunity to make that milk available to every "lamb" who enters my sphere of influence.

Secondly He said, "Take care of my sheep." Sheep are full grown, but in need of constant maintenance to prevent disease or injury. They need to be kept from wandering into danger, or foundering with no one to help them up. Foundering happens when a sheep accidentally rolls into a depression, ending up on its back with its feet in the air, unable to get up because of excess fat or wool. A helpless position indeed! The spiritual applications there are numerous.

How can I, as a fellow sheep, look out for others in the flock? That's where the Body of Christ comes in. God calls me to care for others with whatever skill or insight He has put at my disposal. I pray my brothers and sisters will do the same for me when they find me with hooves pointed skyward!

Thirdly Christ said, "Feed my sheep." How can I nourish other sheep in the flock? I'm sure that answer is different for every one of us since we are gifted so uniquely. For me it means writing encouraging notes and articles, teaching Bible Studies, playing my clarinet in church, taking in meals, loaning my favorite books to others, and giving homemade goodies.

And then Jesus said to Peter, "Follow me!" Perhaps that is the hardest instruction of all. For Peter, it meant stretching out his hands and being led where he did not want to go. Many scholars think this was a prophecy of his later crucifixion. Sometimes the "Follow me" means going into unknown territory, learning new skills, doing dirty, tiresome work that receives no praise, no raise, no bonus… at least not here. But if we die with Christ to our selfish desires, we will also surely follow Him into the resurrected life.

Lord Jesus, Great Shepherd
of the sheep, enable me to
follow you. I do love you.
Help me love you more.
Show me how to feed the
lambs in my care here at
home this week. Use me to
care for and feed the sheep of
your flock in the fellowship
of believers. Most of all,
keep my eyes on you, dear
Lord, so I can follow you to
the end. Amen.

 Soaking
UP HIS SCENT

*Now thanks be to God who always leads us in
triumph in Christ, and through us diffuses the
fragrance of His knowledge in every place. For we
are to God the fragrance of Christ among those who
are being saved and among those who are perishing.
To the one we are the aroma of death leading to
death, and to the other the aroma of life leading to
life. And who is sufficient for these things?*
2 Corinthians 2:14-16 (NKJV)

It was a pleasantly warm summer morning. A perfect day to paint the porch railing. So I pulled on my painting clothes, papered and masked off the porch area and went to work.

The sunshine felt good on my head and back as I worked, and I hummed along with the radio by my side. But as the sun warmed the porch I became aware of the enticing aroma of cinnamon. I knew it wasn't the paint or any of the flowers in the surrounding flower beds. As the scent continued to increase, so did my curiosity of its origin.

Finally, I realized with a laugh that it was my painting outfit! I had stored a bag of cinnamon potpourri next to my workclothes in the closet. The clothes had soaked up the essence of cinnamon, and the warmth of my body and the sun were releasing the aroma in ever increasing strength.

How like Jesus. The closer we get to Him the more we soak up the essence of Christ, and when we go out into the world (when we experience a little heat), His fragrance is what people breathe in. Just as mint leaves when they are crushed give off their scent, so a Christian releases the scent of Christ when he is bruised, if Christ is indeed within.

To some, this whiff of Christ is exotic perfume—the scent of baking bread, spiced cider, brownies fresh from the oven. The truth of Him is a smell so rich it satisfies their deepest hunger. Jesus is life and hope.

To others, Christ is the smell of putrifying flesh, an outhouse in the summer, a rotten egg. Their senses have been distorted by the enemy of Christ. The greatest offering of love that has ever been made available smells to them of death and accusation.

I pray that however He is perceived by those around me, I will be a faithful representative of Christ, not a counterfeit perfume, but one with Him in purpose and spirit.

After I leave my quiet place of devotion, do I carry into the schoolroom the essence of Christ? Do my children sense on me the lingering perfume of God's love? I want to get close enough to Jesus to soak up His scent, like the lingering of my husband's cologne after a good hug and kiss in the morning.

Dear God, you are so precious to me, like the scent of gardenia, so rich you fill a longing deep in my soul. I desire you, Jesus. I ache to know you, be filled with you, be like you. Help me to nestle so close to you that everywhere I go there will be a waft of your perfume in the air. In Jesus' Name, Amen.

November

GIVING THANKS

Your Love
IS EVER BEFORE ME

Test me, O LORD, and try me,
examine my heart and my mind;
for your love is ever before me,
and I walk continually in your truth.
Psalm 26:2-3

After reading these verses in June of 1996, I wrote this in my journal:

"I am fearful to face the testing, examining Spirit of God." But the very next verse says His love is always before me. That makes it less fearsome. To be examined by a loving God makes all the difference, He who knows the intent of my heart.

"Oh, what a blessed relief that He who looks into my deepest soul, looks at me with love!"

"When God tests me, He *wants* to find what is good and pure. He looks at me in love and sees what I want to be in my heart, regardless of the many flaws in my performance."

Our children feel the same way when they face discipline from us. My girls are much more willing to confess a wrong when I am loving and approachable than when I lecture or punish them in anger. Being scrutinized for flaws is a scary thing. If they sense trouble they will avoid me to get around the consequences.

One day Launa came to me in the posture of humility.

"Mommy," she said, "you know when you went in to take Tara's temperature and I was working on my math?"

"Yes," I answered.

"Well, I didn't want to do some of the problems , so... I whited them out."

I tried not to smile at her creative solution. Her sister had been sick for almost a week and she was feeling left out and overburdened, as the only kid in the classroom, and the only one doing chores and piano practice. "Thank you for telling me the truth." I said. "We'll figure out what to do about your math in a few minutes."

I could tell she was infinitely relieved to get the lie out of the way and be forgiven. She hadn't approached me when I was still upset about spilling oatmeal all over Tara's bed and carpet, and in the middle of my rush to get her started with school. Launa waited until she could feel my tenderness toward her.

How wonderful that we serve a God whose love always goes before us. Before He examines us, he loves us. He is never too angry to hear "our side of the story," or to let us sob our frustrations and disappointment in ourselves. He waits until we are ready to listen before He tenderly, but firmly, deals with the sin in our lives.

He is always fair. God doesn't let us off easy just because He knows we mean well. Sin must still be dealt with. But it is weeded out with love, like a gardener carefully removing the weeds hiding in His flower bed. He knows the weeds will choke out the life of the flowers if left to grow.

What a model for us as home school teachers.

When we test or examine our children's work, when we discipline, as we explain a difficult concept—does our love go before correction? If we can convey that love to our children, it may mean the difference between a willing student, ready to listen to instruction (perhaps even asking for advice), and a hardened heart and closed mind.

Dear Heavenly Father, I know I can come to you with any problem, because you have proven your love for me. Help me follow your example and truly love my children. Some days I test and examine without showing love for my children first by touching them, looking in their eyes, and listening to them. Without love the results are disastrous. Show me your ways, Oh Lord, and I will walk continually in your truth. Amen.

Joy-filled THANKS

*Whatever you do, work at it
with all your heart,
as working for the Lord, not for men.*

Colossians 3:23

I learned a lesson from our girls the day I asked them to write thank you notes for the Christmas gifts they had received. I expected them to pull out some stationery and write a few words to each person about their gift. Instead, I witnessed joyful abandon in creative thanksgiving.

They spent the entire morning cutting, gluing, composing and printing—their very best efforts for each individual. One note was shaped like a teapot, another a teddy bear (if you used your imagination), one a tassled purse with a message inside, and another a deep blue card with a splashy, yellow banner announcing, "Thank You So Much!"

It took my breath away to see all the time and energy they gave to this "job." I couldn't bear to tell them the teapot was too big for the envelope, or that I hadn't meant for them to get out all the art supplies for this activity. Instead, I praised them for their whole-hearted obedience and the love they poured into each note (and thanked God we didn't have to go anywhere that morning).

I have to admit I don't always obey my Father that way when He asks me to do something for Him. Sometimes I rush to get it done instead of taking my time and doing it well. I do only what I think is expected, instead of adding a creative flair to make something fresh and new and lovely. I do the job because I have to, not necessarily to bless others.

I would like to take what I learned from my students back into the classroom. Too many times I throw together lesson plans because I have to, instead of setting aside enough time to prepare for the week ahead. I don't always encourage questions and discussion from the girls when they show extra interest because it would "throw us off schedule."

It wouldn't be a bad idea to add creative flair when I grade papers, or dress up the schoolroom with seasonal decorations. In the past I surprised the girls with a fun theme every once in awhile—Teddy Bear Day, Backwards Day, Doll Day, Weird Hair Day, and Pajama Day. It's been months since I brought any lighthearted fun into our schoolroom.

Why am I working so hard to do this job right anyway? Is it just to get them educated and be done with it, or am I teaching them to put a blessing on their lives?

When I lift my thanksgiving to God for all His blessings, He infuses me with energy to be a blessing in our classroom. A thankful heart, then, must be the key to serving Him well, and serving Him creatively.

*Oh Lord, thank you for
reminding me what real giving
is. Help me see the work you
have for me as a joy-filled
challenge. Help me focus on one
job at a time. As I plan lessons
and work with my children, and
whatever else you would have me
do this week, I want to give it
my all. May I work to please
you. The results may not
always be exactly what you had
in mind, but I pray you will be
happy with my efforts and my
attitude. I want to be a delight
to you, Lord. Amen.*

A Reason
TO SING

They will celebrate your
abundant goodness
and joyfully sing of your
righteousness.
Psalm 145:7

A story is told that in the year 200 A.D. an edict went throughout the Roman Empire that all people were to vow allegiance to Caesar as Lord. All those serving in the Imperial Army were required to worship him as deity. One cohort marching across Northern Italy had forty born again believers who refused to obey the order. "We are Christians," they explained to their captain, "and can worship no one but God."

The captain didn't know what to do with these rebels and went to his superior, a man who hated Christians and was only too glad to take the matter into his own hands. He told the men that they would renounce Christ, or face death in the alps of the Apian Way.

That night, as temperatures dipped below zero they were stripped of their clothes and placed out on the icy glacier to "think about it." If they recanted, they could join the others at the fire, if not, they would perish. What did they do? They began to sing.

"Forty brave soldiers for Christ," they sang, huddled together as best they could, "We are forty brave soldiers for Christ," louder and louder until their voices reverberated throughout the valley. This went on for some time, but one of the men could stand it no longer. He stood and said, "Caesar is Lord," and ran for the warmth and comfort of the fire.

There was a moment of silence, then they began again. "Thirty-nine brave soldiers for Christ. We are thirty-nine…"

"No wait!" Their captain looked at them with

tears in his eyes. He glanced one last time at the fire and jumped up, stripped off his clothes, and ran to join his men on the ice. *"Forty* brave soldiers for Christ. We are forty brave soldiers for Christ!" Their song had won his heart. He died with them that night.

Years later in Poland, during the Second World War, another man showed his faith in the Auschwitz concentration camp. Maximilian Kolbe had been arrested for his faith along with two other priests from the friary. But that didn't stop him from showing God's love to others when he entered the concentration camp. Despite the hard work and small rations, Maximilian often gave his food away and prayed with the discouraged.

One day the inmates were told to line up. Someone had escaped and the commander was going to choose ten men to die in the death cell as payment. Numbers, not names, were announced. One man sobbed uncontrollably when his number was called, "My wife, my children!"

Someone was stirring through the ranks of emaciated men, and Maximilian Kolbe stepped to the front of the group. The guards raised their automatic rifles, their dogs were at the ready. "Herr Kommandant, I wish to make a request, please," Maximilian said. "I want to die in place of this prisoner." The man looked up with a mixture of amazement and hope. The commander was for a moment speechless. Then, with a nod, he agreed.

The group of men were marched to the death cell where they were stripped, and locked inside a small hut to watch each other die of starvation. But this time there were not the usual cries of terror and agony. This time there was singing. Maximilian Kolbe was the last to die. He sang the others through the hours of agony, then breathed his last. [1]

In the Middle Ages a saint named Soetgen, from Ghent, Belgium, wrote these words in one of her last letters to her children before she was burned at the stake: "Since it pleases the Lord to take me out of this world, I will leave you a memorial, not of silver or gold; for such jewels are perishable: but I should like to write a jewel into your heart, if it were possible, which is the word of truth." [2]

May we impart to our children this treasure of faith, giving each of us a reason to sing, no matter what the circumstances.

Dear God, after reading these stories my faith seems small indeed. Help me sing in good times and bad, because you, Oh Lord, are a jewel beyond compare and worthy to be praised. Help me see the importance of keeping music in our curriculum, because it can touch our hearts and refresh us in times of need like nothing else can. May the truth shine forth and give us all a reason to sing. Amen.

Shouting
WITH JOY

At his tabernacle will I sacrifice
with shouts of joy;
I will sing and make music to the
LORD.
Psalm 27:6b

I have always thought of sacrificing as such a solemn ritual, and yet David talks about sacrificing with shouts of joy and singing. Do I worship that way—with joy, shouts, and singing spontaneously? Do I sacrifice that way—giving my best offering to God with overflowing love and praise?

I have to admit I'm a rather quiet worshiper in church, but on the rare occasion I have time at home by myself I enjoy singing and praising God with abandon, when no one is watching. But when it comes to sacrificing (doing without), the only noises I tend to make are whining and complaining.

For me, home schooling has been the ultimate sacrifice—giving to God and our children years for which I had other plans. I didn't initially make that sacrifice with a happy face, and not with shouts of joy. There was no music or singing to begin with. But God took that sacrifice, grudgingly given, and in His mercy, blessed us to overflowing.

Now the joy, music, and laughter has come. I wish I had trusted more and rejoiced from the start. It has been a hard lesson to learn.

What, for you, is a sacrifice—time, money, service, words of encouragement and love, physical touch? Are you willing to release this to God with a joyful heart, knowing that He will accept that sacrifice as a sign of your devotion to Him? Do you sing, dance, and make music before Him?

Sometimes our best sacrifice to God is when we are willing to give our children and spouse the things they need most. Often those are the most difficult things to give. Perhaps it doesn't come naturally to us; we don't see the need for it; we're too tired. That's what makes it a worthwhile gift to our Lord, when we give anyway, to please Him.

David said, "I will not sacrifice to the LORD my God burnt offerings that cost me nothing" (2 Samuel 24:24). One definition of the word sacrifice is to forfeit something of high value for the sake of someone you consider to have greater value, or claim to it. Who has greater value than God? Who has more of a claim to everything we have, and everything we are than He? King David did not take God for granted; he was willing to pay the price. Are we?

Oh Lord, I want to have
a willing heart to give to you
this week. May I sacrifice my
time with joyful songs, my
words lifted to you in worship,
my hands and body working
out the music of praise to you
as I teach and in all I do. May
they be pure and unblemished
offerings, a pleasing aroma
rising to you. Amen.

December

PRAISING GOD

All
FOR THE GLORY OF GOD

So whether you eat or drink or whatever you do,
do it all for the glory of God.

1 Corinthians 10:31

How does my attitude toward food, as
a Christian, affect others' perception of God? Is He
being glorified by the way I talk about it, use it, or
go without?

I have a history of food addiction. I don't
vacillate, as the Corinthians did, whether or not to
eat food that has been offered to idols. I struggle
whether or not to eat chocolate three times a day as
I'd like, or to eat the dessert offered at Bible Study
when my pants are already too tight and I know
I need to lose a few pounds. I haven't binged for
a long time, but still tend to think of food as
a companion, a place to bury my sorrows, something
to celebrate with, a forbidden delight, and secret joy.
So in a way it boils down to the same thing about
which Paul spoke to the Corinthians.

Perhaps this is not an area of difficulty for
you, but I have a suspicion it is for many. Our
society today is obsessed by food—choosing it,
eating it, going without, getting the taste without
suffering the effects. We either feel pious about our
ultra healthy, low fat, low cal, high fiber diets and
regular fast days. Or we are riddled with guilt about
how much processed sugar and flour we consume,
and find ourselves settling for packaged or fast food,
because it's easier after teaching all day.

So what's the answer? Neither a pious
attitude nor guilt is glorifying to God. Either attitude

harms our witness to the unsaved, both distance us from others, and neither is a heritage we want to pass on to our children.

The issue is why do we eat what we do, and how does it affect our relationship with God and others? As believers we have the freedom to eat however we want. The three stipulations Paul gave the Corinthians were: 1. We shouldn't eat selfishly, 2. Our eating shouldn't cause anyone else to stumble, and 3. It should glorify God.

Selfish behaviors include overeating, hoarding, and eating to please ourselves. " 'Everything is permissible'—but not everything is beneficial. 'Everything is permissible'—but not everything is constructive. Nobody should seek his own good, but the good of others." (1 Cor. 10:23-24)

Another way of being selfish is expecting everyone to bow to the diet we have chosen, rejecting another's hospitality because it doesn't fit our regime. Instead, we should thankfully eat portions of what is put before us without fussing about content.

The second consideration is found in verse 32—whether our eating or attitude would cause someone else to stumble. Our words and actions may cause our children to develop unhealthy attitudes about food, or unrealistic expectations of how their bodies should look. This is a very real threat in today's world. We are inundated by the media's portrayal of the "perfect image." Even home schooled children are touched by this.

The third rule is actually an umbrella that covers all situations—"so whether you eat or drink or whatever you do, do it all for the glory of God." Everything we do should be done for the good of others, to keep them from stumbling, and bring glory to God. We can help our children learn this truth as we teach them healthy eating habits for life in the classroom and at the table.

(An excellent resource for finding a balanced approach to eating: *The Weigh Down Diet* by Gwen Shamblin)

Dear God, this is a big issue for me. I am not there yet, you know that. Too often I eat, or don't eat, out of selfishness. Help me have a healthy attitude about food and be thankful for the rich provisions you have given us on this earth. Help me model this for our children and pass on a legacy of godliness instead of slavery to diets or food abuse. Keep me in balance, Lord. May all my habits bring glory to you. In Jesus' Name, Amen.

Excel
IN GIVING

But just as you excel in everything—
in faith, in speech, in knowledge,
in complete earnestness and in your love for
us—see that you also
excel in this grace of giving.
2 Corinthians 8:7

The day had been a success. Our Friday School co-op had made dozens of sugar cookies and valentines to give to widows and widowers from our churches and neighborhoods. It was time to pack it in and go deliver the goods. But when I informed my girls it was time to go, they were less than enthusiastic.

"Girls," I called, "it's time to get your plates and choose the cookies you want to give for Valentines," I said.

The response was lethargic, but eventually Launa chose six cookies without any frosting and plunked them down on a plate. I told her those were the leftovers for us to eat, the frosted ones were for giving. Launa looked at me like I'd just shot her best friend. Tara told me she had decorated cookies and given them away to her friends at Friday school. She didn't want to give away cookies someone else had decorated.

I was embarrassed and angry. Here we had spent all day in preparation for this moment and my children didn't have a clue what we were doing! I began to lecture them about how important it is for us to show love to widows and widowers who might be feeling especially lonely on Valentines Day. Redfaced and sullen, we gathered some decorated cookies onto plates and left to make our deliveries.

Praise God for His grace. None of us had the right attitude, but He made it into a joyous occasion anyway. We arrived at the office of a recent widower from our church and our excitement began to mount. Unbeknownst to him, we had conspired with his secretary to deliver goodies to him there. When he saw us, tears welled up in his eyes and he hugged each of us, praising God for His faithfulness. He sampled a cookie, hugged us each again, talked about his wife and grandchildren, pouring out love and gratitude. Then he hugged us once again before we left. As we were leaving I asked, "Now, aren't you glad you didn't give him a plate of plain sugar cookies?"

Launa's eyes widened and she nodded. "He needed those cookies a lot more than we did!" It was a learning experience for all of us. We know now how much more we need to practice giving to others and, sometimes, how hard it is to let go of the goods.

Our co-op planned another give away activity for May Day. It went much better that time (maybe because we gave away flowers instead of cookies). The children wrapped potted flowers and gave them to residents in a local retirement home. We came away feeling tired, but pleased that our efforts delighted God and brought cheer to many that day.

Giving can be hard. Thinking about giving is easy—ideas come on wings. But as Paul reminded the believers in Corinth, you have to plan ahead and

then carry out that plan according to your means.
(2 Corinthians 8:11-12)

As home schoolers, we excel in teaching our children about God, how to respect others, and share their faith. Many are ranked first in the nation academically. We earnestly pray our children will become strong believers. It's also important to excel in giving to others whenever possible—giving time, money, effort, sincere prayer… and cookies.

Dear Lord, this is an area we need to work on more in our home. Community projects are wonderful, but we need to develop an attitude of giving in all of life. May our love for you overflow in generosity to others. Everything we have belongs to you. Help us to hold onto these things lightly, in case our brother or sister might have a greater need for them than we. Amen.

Shining
EVER BRIGHTER

*The path of the righteous is like
the first gleam of dawn,
shining ever brighter till the
full light of day.*
Proverbs 4:18

During the winter months it is dark when I get up. The house is still. I slip downstairs to make a cup of coffee before coming up to my quiet place to begin the day with God. Darkness is not a friendly invitation to get out of my warm bed, but I'm not quite ready to turn on a bunch of bright lights first thing in the morning either.

That's why I like to have a small lamp beside my reading corner. It shines warmth and light into the gloom of early morning. As the sun comes up, the greater light slowly fills the room and I am ready to greet the light of day.

That is our life as Christians; we are a lamp in the darkness. The world is not ready to face the glory of God in a sudden burst of light. It would be blinding, terrifying, as Daniel and John in the Bible testified after seeing visions of God. Psalm 76:4 says, He is "resplendent with light." That's why He uses us to draw people to Him.

We are the first gleam of dawn—a lamp that makes God's coming attractive and inviting, as those around us are ready to see more of Him. As we grow in our own relationship with God, He shows more and more of His light, until the full light of day, the day when God himself will appear.

More than anything, of course, we want to be a light to our children. They could be living in darkness, even in a loving Christian home. But with a few "strategically placed" lamps around (otherwise known as Mom and Dad, brothers and sisters), they may begin to see the light.

Isaiah 60:1-3 says, " 'Arise, shine, for your light has come, and the glory of the LORD rises upon you... See, darkness covers the earth and thick darkness is over the peoples, but the LORD rises upon you and his glory appears over you. Nations will come to your light, and kings to the brightness of your dawn.' "

I must constantly ask myself, "Is my light shining to everyone in the house? Does it include all my family members, as well as children who come to play, and guests in our home?" There's not much time left, I believe, to make the light known. Romans 13:12 says, "The night is nearly over; the day is almost here. So let us put aside the deeds of darkness and put on the armor of light."

Our light is nothing in comparison to God's light, but He graciously allows us to be vessels for Him until His coming, to shine forth in the darkness. But in heaven our work as lamps will be over. There will be no darkness. All will be light: "The city does not need the sun or the moon to shine on it, for the glory of God gives it light, and the Lamb is its lamp. The nations will walk by its light, and the kings of the earth will bring their splendor into it" (Rev. 21:23-24) and "There will be no more night. They will not need the light of a lamp or the light of the sun, for the Lord God will give them light. And they will reign for ever and ever." (Rev. 22:5)

How can we shine for Him brighter every day? We must stay on the path of righteousness, not the path of church work, or scholastic achievement, or scripture memorization, but the path of faith. God, in whose light we see light, will illuminate our lives and shine into a world hungry for Him.

Dear God, I long to see more of your light. Sometimes I feel like I am in darkness. All I can see is a pinprick of light. Bring me closer to your glory, Lord, so I can know your splendor and majesty. Infuse me with your light. Help me to shine with a brightness that draws others to you. Help me be a light to my children this week, in school and out. Amen.

Why
I TEACH

Pay attention and listen to the sayings of the wise;
apply your heart to what I teach,
for it is pleasing when you keep them in your heart
and have all of them ready on your lips.
So that your trust may be in the LORD,
I teach you today, even you.
Have I not written thirty sayings for you,
sayings of counsel and knowledge,
teaching you true and reliable words,
so that you can give sound answers
to him who sent you?
Proverbs 22:17-21

These were our theme verses for the 1997-98 year. First we memorized them and talked about what it means to listen and apply the lessons we learn in school. Then I kept them posted in our classroom to remind myself why I teach our girls at home. There are two main reasons: 1. So that their trust may be in the Lord, and 2. So they can give sound answers.

One argument Tara used when she was trying to convince me to home school her, after attending first grade in public school, was, "I want to be able to talk about Jesus. We can't do that in public school, Mom." *(She knew that would get me.)*

At home, we are free to set up our day any way we please, giving whatever time is necessary for each subject. Some days our devotion time is only 30 minutes, but other days it stretches into an hour when there are special problems to discuss or questions that need to be answered. We will often spend extra time interceding for a special need, or singing "just one more song" when we need an extra spark of joy to begin our day.

I'm aware of the girls' ploy to make devotions last a little longer in order to cheat math time, but I say with Paul, "what does it matter? The important thing is that in every way, whether from false motives or true, Christ is preached. And because of this I rejoice." (Phil. 1:18)

That's our highest aim, beyond equipping them with a fine education, sound thinking skills, good manners, and the ability to communicate with others. Above all else, we long for our girls to leave home with their hand in the hand of God. To see them leave home trusting in Him and following His leadership all their lives would be our greatest joy.

Secondly, we want them to be able to give sound answers. The teacher in Proverbs 22 wanted his student to be able to give sound answers to the one who sent him (probably his parents). Our children will also be questioned about what they've learned.

I want Launa and Tara to be able to answer people when asked about their faith, as 1 Peter 3:15 says, "Always be prepared to give an answer to everyone who asks you to give the reason for the hope that you have." I pray that the layering of truths from God's Word will make sense to their minds and hearts, and that they will be able to explain their relationship with Him simply to others.

Beyond that, we want them to have a sound answer to give to the One who sent them here in the first place—their Heavenly Father. They will one day stand before the Throne to give an account of their lives. May all that we have taught them contribute to their assurance of salvation on that Day. That would make it all worthwhile.

My Lord, the responsibility seems overwhelming at times, but I must remember I am only answerable for my own obedience, not my children's. With your help I can equip them, but I know they must choose whether or not they will use that knowledge to serve you. Help us do all we can to lead our children to faith in you, and to be able to explain their faith to others. Help me focus on what's most important this week. Amen.

January

THE WINTER FREEZE

Daily

Praise be to the Lord, to God our Savior,
who daily bears our burdens.
Psalm 68:19

This verse makes me want to sing! It's the little stuff that seems to get me down, and that word "daily" is such a comfort. Yesterday had its own set of problems and today is new and fresh and full of another set of burdens to be carried. But every time I release a problem to my Savior, He lifts the load from my shoulders and my fretting mind and carries it for me. I can trust Him to do that.

I am mistaken when I think that any problem is too small for Him. Truly, God gives us salvation, courage to withstand the enemy, endure persecution, and shine His light into the darkness. But He also wants to empower us in the little things that encumber and depress.

When I was in the eighth grade I played clarinet in the band and alto saxophone in Jazz Band. Every morning I carried my clarinet case and books in the crook of my left arm and my saxophone in my right hand. I carried them onto the bus in the morning, off the bus to my locker through the crowded halls to band practice, back to my locker, and back home each night. What I would have given for a friend to help me carry around all my stuff!

These days the "stuff" I carry around is mostly on the inside. And I have found a Friend who's willing to help me. Yesterday I gave Him the burden of my headache and fatigue after the previous day's fieldtrip. I gave Him frayed nerve endings and PMS knots. I gave Him our daughters—one suffering with preteen emotions, and one that would rather play than concentrate on school work. I asked for wisdom, "How can I work through my own weaknesses, Lord, and teach each child according to her needs with patience and gentleness?"

Today, the burdens weighing me down are a little different. Today I have some time off. How can I use it wisely? I want to accomplish the maximum amount of work in the minimum of time. But then, there is the "burden" of needing to be quiet and rest too. I decided to give God my "list" and ask Him to guide my steps according to His plan.

There are days I'm completely overwhelmed by the very same things I've carried easily on other days. Perhaps the circumstances are different, or my physical or emotional capabilities weakened. Jesus understands that and lifts the weight from my back without chiding me for my lack of strength.

Are you trying to carry too much today? Do you need a Friend to help you?

Dear God, thank you for being willing not only to carry the cross for me—certainly a burden I never could have borne—but that you also come alongside me each day to bear my burdens. Life can get so heavy at times. Here are the things that are weighing me down. Lord, help me walk trustingly with you, unencumbered by these worries. Amen.

Energizing
POWER

It is God Who energizeth within you,
both the desiring and the energizing,
in behalf of His good pleasure. All things be doing,
apart from murmurings and disputings.
Philippians 2:13-14 (Rotherham)

Philippians 2:13 first became a special verse to me when my husband and I lived in Kansas City. Jeff had felt God's call to do something more for Him and wanted to volunteer through our church for a year. Having already moved halfway across the country the day after college graduation, I was in no mood to go into "missionary" work. It had taken me more than a year to get used to married life and my new environment. I thrashed against the very idea.

But it was evident God was working in Jeff's heart. I knew I had to pray. But pray for what? I didn't want to pray against God's leading if this was His will, but at the same time, I felt no call. Then I read Philippians 2:13 in my devotions, "For it is God who works in you to will and to act according to his good purpose."

"Lord," I prayed, "if this is something you want us to do, help me be willing. You know this is not my desire. But I know you can change my heart. Please show me what your good purpose for us is."

It didn't take long before my heart began to change. I can't say I suddenly had a yearning to go into deepest Africa to face the natives, but I was willing to find out more about the volunteer program. Eventually, we ended up spending a year in the "jungle" of New York, remodeling a church building—a wonderful year of adventure, friendship, miracles, growth, and great joy.

That was in 1986. In 1996 I rediscovered Philippians 2:13 in Amy Carmichael's writings. Amy Carmichael, missionary to India, read from many different translations of the Bible, gleaning as much as possible for her own spiritual growth and in order to bless others. In her devotional, *Edges of His Ways*, she referred to Philippians 2:13-14: "Have you ever connected these two verses? I do not think I ever did till today when I read from the one straight into the other... this means we must not ask for easy things for each other. We must rather pray that we shall be so gloriously energized by the mighty power of God, that we shall do all things that come to be done, without a single inward grumble, making them our pleasure because they are His good pleasure." [3]

I then wrote in my journal, "What is this human frailty that causes us always to seek the comfortable way, the easy path? God never called us to pray that way. Jesus never taught us to pray for ease. Lord, help us to change our prayers from, 'lighten my load' to 'make my back strong!' "

"Along with a stronger back, plus the power and energy to do your will, grant me an attitude that never murmurs or complains against you, my Master, Sovereign of all my days. Purify my attitude, oh God. I need to be cleansed of selfishness and self-pity." (June 11, 1996)

Amy's devotional emphasized God's energizing power—power to be willing, power to act according to God's good purpose, power to do it without complaining or arguing. That's what we need in our home and in our school.

I know God's energizing power is more than coping medication. It's better than a cup of coffee to pry open my lids and give me a push into the day. God's Holy

Spirit-filled, energizing power is a constant flow of His being pouring through my heart, mind, spirit and will. That's what I need each day. I don't think I have begun to tap into what God has for me.

I am beginning to pray for God's energizing power in each family member's life as we face tests and trials. We need to know God's energizing power can help us desire what is right, and to do His will, and to do it without complaint, even the things that seem impossible.

My Lord and my God, I am slow to learn. It hurts to admit there are times when I don't even want to do your will. I have to back up and pray for you to give me the right desires, even before I can receive your help in doing what you ask. And then, when I am willing and do what you ask, sometimes I grumble and complain. Forgive me, Lord. Please have mercy on me and help me to be more like Jesus. Energize me by your Spirit. Help me pray for this kind of power in others as well, that we might become a people of power and joy in you. Amen.

Stones
OF REMEMBRANCE

"And Joshua set up at Gilgal the twelve stones they had taken out of the Jordan. He said to the Israelites, 'In the future when your descendants ask their fathers, "What do these stones mean?" tell them, 'Israel crossed the Jordan on dry ground.' For the LORD your God dried up the Jordan before you until you had crossed over... He did this so that all the peoples of the earth might know that the hand of the LORD is powerful and so that you might always fear the LORD your God."

Joshua 4:20-24

It is no accident that yesterday the special speaker at our church talked from this very passage about stones of remembrance. I have had this scripture entered on my computer for some time. I didn't know I would be working on this particular devotion today. But God knew.

He knew what an impact the sermon would have on my heart. God knew I would be reviewing what the pastor said in my quiet time this morning and excitedly looking through journals to get dates and facts for our Stones of Remembrance box.

It wasn't until yesterday when David Miller, president of Western Baptist College, spoke at our church, that I ever thought about taking this scripture so literally. He said if there was anything he could have done differently in raising his four boys, he would have piled rocks in the living room, rocks in their backyard, rocks in their bedrooms. And when his sons asked, "Why all the rocks, Dad?" he would say, "Sit down, son. I've got a story to tell you about the miracles God has done in my life…"

In fact, he has been doing that very thing in recent years. They have huge rocks in the backyard of their new home (one of the reasons they decided to buy that particular house), he has rocks on his desk, and rocks in the trophy case of the athletic department. And every time someone asks, "Why all the rocks?" he says, "Sit down. I've got a story to tell you…"

Being a rock lover, I have always wanted a valid excuse for collecting beautiful, polished rocks. Now I have one. (Who says God doesn't give us the desires of our heart?) This morning I began to write down dates of the big events of our lives. I wrote the years Jeff and I gave our hearts to Christ, and looked through the journals I keep for our girls to find the dates of their conversions. I added our wedding date, the days our girls were born, and other life changing events, full of God's grace. Now all we need are the rocks.

Each one will be labeled for our Memory Box. Eventually, I would like to purchase a hand-made, wooden box for these treasures and have Joshua 4:6-7 written on it, "In the future, when your children ask you, 'What do these stones mean?' tell them… These stones are to be a memorial."

What child doesn't like to look at and handle beautiful, smooth, or glittery rocks? And each rock represents a story. What child doesn't like stories, especially if he is the main character? These rocks tell the story of their life, their heritage — a way to remember God's goodness.

How like God to take the natural curiosity of a child and turn it into a blessing. The reason God instructed the Israelites to pile up rocks after crossing the Jordan on dry land was so the record of His love could be passed on from generation to generation. We have short memories. God knows that. He knows we need visual reminders so we don't forget the miracles He has done for us, and, so we have a natural opportunity to pass it on to our children.

This is something that could be done together in the classroom or as a family. Even young children can think of milestones in your family history and help choose what kind of memorial to use. You may not be rock lovers. That's OK. What will your "stones of remembrance" be? They could be teacups, plants for the yard, pictures in a special album. Whatever you choose to help you remember God's goodness to you, He will bless your family for honoring Him.

Holy God, I have thought about this concept for some time. Now you have given me exciting ideas to carry out. Help us honor you with this memorial. May our stones of remembrance draw us together as a family and give our children a sense of your care for us. It's so easy to forget all the miracles you've done in our family, especially when things aren't going well. I pray these objects will cause our children to ask questions and keep the memories fresh, so we won't fail to tell future generations what you've done for us. Amen.

Peace
WITHIN YOUR BORDERS

For he strengthens the bars of your gates
and blesses your people within you.
He grants peace to your borders.
Psalm 147:13-14

What a beautiful blessing we can claim for our homes! Written as a prayer for Jerusalem, it is also the prayer of our hearts as home schoolers. Yes, Lord, strengthen the bars of our gates, bless the members of our families, and grant peace within the borders of our home. We need to protect our young ones while teaching them biblical principles, strengthening their spirits, and helping them develop intellect and character.

And yet, there are times when I feel hemmed in by the very borders we have established. I see our girls thriving in the home environment, free from some of the outside pressures on their time, beliefs, and behavior. But I struggle with my borders sometimes.

There are days when I long for the freedom I see other women enjoying—time to shop, meet a friend for lunch, read something other than a textbook. Sometimes I wish I could attend a daytime Bible Study, go to aerobics, or get the house clean. On days like this I begin to rail at the borders which once seemed so friendly. They begin to look like prison walls, especially in these winter months.

That is when I seek the face of the only One who can show me how to be at peace within these walls. He reminds me the reasons they are there—protection, beauty, definition, strength, security. These reasons point me in the right direction again with a sense of purpose.

To my surprise, He also shows me places to expand my borders a little. I had planted a hedge of impossible expectations around us all—scholastic, housecleaning, community, church activities, and ministry. There was no room for us to play and explore. How freeing to realize it's OK if I take a little time to do the things I enjoy.

Parenting can be an overwhelming task at times, and a teaching parent can feel even more imprisoned by the greatness of the task. My prayer for you is that God will grant peace to your borders this week. May He strengthen the walls that need to be there and help you expand in areas where perhaps you haven't allowed enough space for yourself or your family. May He protect you from the evil one and delight you with joy.

Dear God, I don't know why
I struggle like this at times, but
I do, and you are the only One
who can give me peace.
Sometimes the walls close in on
me. Am I being selfish, or do I need
to be refreshed? Show me your
way. I long to break free of these
confines, and yet... my children
need this safe place to grow and
become. Help me accept your peace
and provision in this place and
rejoice in your blessings on our
home school this week. Amen.

February

WHAT I NEED TO BE

He Cares
FOR THE CAREGIVER

He tends his flock like a shepherd:
He gathers the lambs in his arms
and carries them close to his heart;
he gently leads those that have young.
Isaiah 40:11

This verse has comforted me many times. The Good Shepherd does not drive a flock hard when there are young lambs. The little ones wouldn't be able to keep up and the sheep would be in distress. Instead He carries the littlest ones himself, close to His loving heart. And He gently encourages the mothers on their way. So why is it that we drive ourselves so hard, causing our own demise?

We add pressures to our lives that God never intended for us to tackle when our children are young. And we do it for a variety of "sensible" reasons: "I must use this curriculum to help our children get the best education they can." "I'll take on this extra job so our children won't have to go without." "No one else at church will do the job, so I'll have to volunteer." "I know my schedule's packed, but this would be a wonderful opportunity." "I'm so tired, but I feel like I should…"

How many of those things have you said to yourself just before embarking on an adventure in stressful living? This is not to say God does not sometimes lead us down paths that are difficult, to add muscle to our faith. But too often we make life harder than it need be. It is not His plan to lead a flock of frantic sheep raising up a generation of nervous lambs.

In the Bible God made specific provisions for animals with young, showing His care even for animals raised for food: Don't cook a goat in its mother's milk; don't slaughter an animal and its young on the same day; do not take both a mother bird and its young. (Ex. 23:19, 34:26; Lev. 22:28; Deut. 14:21b, 22:6-7) In other passages He used people's knowledge of animal behavior to describe His love for all creation and His particular tenderness for mankind. (Deut. 32:10-12; Job 38:39-39:8; Ps. 84:3; Is. 40:11; Lam. 4:3-4)

When Jacob met his brother, Esau, on his way home from serving Laban for twenty years, Esau offered to travel together. But Jacob said, "My lord knows that the children are tender and that I must care for the ewes and cows that are nursing their young. If they are driven hard just one day, all the animals will die." (Gen. 33:13) Whether this was completely out of concern for the young or whether Jacob was wary of Esau's offer of friendship is hard to tell. The point is, he considered the needs of his family and flocks.

If God has gone to the trouble to provide good examples of His concern for animals with young, how much more is He concerned with His people, understanding our needs as parents. He promises not to drive us too hard. He leads us to green pastures. He restores our soul. At times He will have to lead us through the shadows, but even then He offers comfort, guidance, and the freshness of new grazing lands.

Do you find yourself going in too many directions? As home educators we must constantly re-evaluate our schedule to keep from becoming too busy. If we're not careful we will wear ourselves and our children out and end up "dying on the way."

I once heard a preacher say that sometimes the holiest thing you can do is take a nap. It doesn't help for us to get so tired and frazzled that we end up doing and saying things we regret. We need to allow our children the rest and free-play time they need as individuals.

Guilt and comparison are two of the greatest enemies to a simple, joy-filled life. It's a challenge to balance service with restoration, activity with rest, but with God as our Shepherd we can find that balance in our homes.

Dear Jesus, Shepherd of the sheep, thank you for being a gentle Shepherd. I forget, as our Creator, you understand our limitations. Forgive me for driving myself and my little ones harder than I should. Help me keep my eyes on you and stop trying to prove to the world that we are the perfect home school family. Show me what is best for us this week and let the rest go for now. Lead us. Carry us close to your heart, I pray. Amen.

His Wisdom
HIS STRENGTH

For the foolishness of God is wiser than man's wisdom,
and the weakness of God is stronger than man's
strength.
Corinthians 1:25

$\mathcal{G}$ideon is one of my favorite characters in the Bible. I guess I can relate to his hesitancy that God could use him to accomplish His will. When the angel of the Lord first appeared to Gideon he was threshing wheat in the confines of a winepress, secreted away from the Midianites. The angel's greeting to him was, "The LORD is with you, mighty warrior." (Judges 6:12)

Isn't that just like God, to see us as we are meant to be, as we will be with His help, rather than as the frightened little rabbit we are at the moment? Gideon surely didn't see himself as a mighty warrior, and he didn't for some time. He needed evidence that it was really him God wanted.

Even after God called him into service, Gideon was afraid to obey in daylight. When he tore down the altar to Baal, he and his men went at night. In the morning everyone was in a dither. It was his father's wisdom that saved Gideon from getting stoned when the men of the town found out who had destroyed their god.

God's hero seemed like a poor choice—the lowest man on the totem pole, from the weakest clan of the Israelites, afraid to act in daylight, needing constant reassurance. Add to these things the "foolishness" of God's battle plan.

The Midianites already outnumbered the Israelites (that's why they had to thresh wheat in secret—to keep it from raiders). But God told Gideon to thin out the Israelite troops from 32,000 to 10,000 men, letting all who were afraid go home (no doubt Gideon wanted to go with them). Then He had Gideon watch the men and send home the ones who put their face in the water to drink, keeping the ones who scooped the water with their hands. There remained a whopping 300 soldiers to defeat the Midianites who had settled in the valley "thick as locusts."

And how were 300 Israelites going to defend their land against so many? With trumpets and jars of course! The foolishness of God's plan was to show that His "weakest" plan is stronger than man's most powerful army. He loves to do the impossible. He didn't want it to look like Israel had a fighting chance, "In order that Israel may not boast against me that her own strength has saved her." (Judges 7:2b)

Do you feel like Gideon: unqualified to teach your children effectively, afraid, setting out fleece after fleece to be sure it's you God wants to use? He understands. God delights in using ordinary people like you and me to defeat the trumped up power of the enemy (pardon the pun). He enjoys a little foolishness to show the world how absurd it is to think any power could defeat Him.

Isn't it wonderful that God is patient with our insecurities and is willing to give us the reassurance we need by speaking to us personally, answering the fleeces we set out before Him, and speaking encouragement to us through others? He knows our weaknesses, but He wants to use us anyway. May He work in us and through us in our schools and homes and communities until He comes for us when the final trumpet sounds.

Dear God, you know my fears. I do not feel worthy to lead your people to victory, even the small group of "soldiers" I have here at home. But you have called me to show how foolishness can be wise and weakness can be strength when you are in charge. Be the commander of our school, Lord. We will follow your instructions. In Jesus' Name, Amen.

Darkness
IS PASSING

Yet I am writing you a new command;
its truth is seen in him and you,
because the darkness is passing and the
true light is already shining.

1 John 2:8

As a child, I had a strange fascination with darkness, and enjoyed exploring fear and sadness to their very depths. One day I lay on my bunkbed in my darkened room, savoring the Edgar Allen Poeishness of the moment, when suddenly the darkness turned on me. I knew I was no longer in control of the storyline; I was not alone. My whispered calls for help in the adventure I had been creating became real cries for help, growing louder with my increasing fear.

I remember seeing the light from the hallway and breathing with relief when my older sister came in to rescue me. She laid me down on the family room couch, and questioned me about what I might have taken or used to produce such alarming results. The bright room and the light emanating from her face flooded over me. I couldn't explain to her at the time, why, without drugs or alcohol, I had acted so irrationally. I had experienced a truer darkness than I had ever known existed.

Over the next few years, God's light shone out to me through my sisters, my parents and others. In the eighth grade I allowed the light of God to penetrate the darkness of my soul. It has been shining ever since. The light is growing stronger, but some days my own self-centeredness dims His light in me and I must seek forgiveness.

The other day I was trying to help our youngest find the right words to communicate with her sister without resorting to hurtful, angry words. When I finished, Tara said, "But you don't do that Mommy."

I wanted to rationalize. I wanted to cry. But she was right, I could say nothing in my defense. I also am a child of God, learning His ways, trying to live in obedience to Him. I had to admit to my girls (what they already knew) that I still blow it sometimes, and let my own feelings get in the way of doing and saying what I know is right.

The good news is that His light is continually penetrating those dark places in me. Often God uses our children to expose those dark corners with a beam of His truth. For if we teach the truth, it will come back to teach us.

I was encouraged when I read the story of Columba, born in Ireland in 521. He had such a fiery temper and stubborn will that what started as an argument between him and a friend, turned into a war that killed 3,000 men. When Columba realized what he had done, he repented and God used it for good. Columba became a missionary to Scotland at the age of 42, vowing to save as many as had died because of him. There he built a monastery for the training of missionaries and converted large numbers. [4]

How I praise God that He not only shows us our sin, but offers the cure, His loving forgiveness. He is willing to flood our lives with His glorious light and show us a better way to live.

Part of our job is to reveal to our children a true picture of the blackness of sin. They need to see their hearts as dark caves of hopelessness without God. They also need to see the hope Jesus brings — He will light up their lives and keep on shining in them with ever increasing light until the darkness of sin and this world have totally passed away.

Lord, I need your light today. I fail so often. My children know my faults. I pray that you will keep shining your light in me, making me more like Jesus. It's hard to be anything but humble with little eyes watching and pointing out my flaws. Help me to humbly accept these rebukes as from you, seeking forgiveness and wisdom and love from your Spirit. Help me teach them by word and example about the light of your love. Amen.

Velvet
COVERED STEEL

A wife of noble character who can find?
She is worth far more than rubies.
Her husband has full confidence in her
and lacks nothing of value.
She brings him good, not harm,
all the days of her life.
She gets up while it is still dark;
she provides food for her family
and portions for her servant girls.
She considers a field and buys it;
out of her earnings she plants a vineyard.
She sets about her work vigorously;
her arms are strong for her tasks.
She sees that her trading is profitable,
and her lamp does not go out at night.
She opens her arms to the poor
and extends her hands to the needy.
When it snows, she has no fear for her household;
for all of them are clothed in scarlet.
She makes coverings for her bed;
she is clothed in fine linen and purple.
She is clothed with strength and dignity;
she can laugh at the days to come.
She speaks with wisdom,
and faithful instruction is on her tongue.
She watches over the affairs of her household
and does not eat the bread of idleness.
Her children arise and call her blessed;
her husband also, and he praises her.

selected verses from Proverbs 31:10-28

Pat Holt and Grace Ketterman, M.D. have written a wonderful book entitled, *When You Feel Like Screaming*. I don't know if you ever feel like screaming, but there are times when I have resorted to it for "crowd control." Holt and Ketterman's answer to maintaining order without becoming a drill sergeant is as follows:

" 'Velvet over steel' is a three-word picture of the mother who is fun-loving, soft, gentle, yet exudes strength and control. The undergirding of strength and control allows her to be fun-loving with her children and even permits her to act silly. She can do it because she is still in control of herself and in control of her children. She knows it and they know it!" [5]

Isn't that exactly what we want to be? The Wife of Noble Character in Proverbs 31 is a Velvet Over Steel woman. Her strength, or steel, is shown in the way she works hard to provide for her family's needs, the no-nonsense way she conducts business, her wise consideration before purchasing, and faithful instruction to her children.

She is covered in velvet as seen in her compassion for the poor. Her family is clothed beautifully (in expensive scarlet, the color associated with nobility), as well as practically. She also takes time to decorate her bedroom beautifully. There is a softness about this lady that draws others. The noble woman's husband is respected in the community and her family members give her love and praise.

This is a challenge indeed. Most of us tend to be either too much velvet or too much unbending steel. I tend to be more steel and need to learn to be soft and approachable. I need to set aside my list sometimes to run, tickle, laugh, and play with my family. I need compassion and patience to listen when they talk. Steel can be hard to snuggle up to.

Perhaps you are one of the beautiful velvet mothers, full of hugs and tenderness. But you find you can't get things done and your children get away with more than they should because of your softness. Do you need some steel under that velvet to run your school and household more effectively?

This is a wonderful model to keep in mind as we teach our children and go about our daily tasks. I pray it is as much of an encouragement to you as it has been to me.

Dear Lord, you know what I am; you know my needs. Some days I don't feel like I'm anywhere near being a woman of noble character. Build in me a frame of steel, willing to do the hard tasks, striving for excellence. Then cover me with the velvet of your loving compassion, your gentle softness to love my family for you. That is how you lived and taught. Let me be a teacher like you. Amen.

March

THERE ARE REWARDS

Resting
IN VICTORY

Even while you sleep among the campfires,
the wings of my dove are sheathed with silver,
its feathers with shining gold.

Psalm 68:13

$\mathcal{D}$on't you wish you could see everything God is doing in the hearts of your children? How your faith and prayers are affecting your neighborhood? How the angels of God are fighting to protect your church, your home, your mind, body, and spirit from Satan and his demons who seek to invade?

So many times we long for eyes to see these spiritual realities, but we cannot see or even comprehend the battles being fought all around us. However, we can rest in faith knowing God is at work, even while we sleep, and reap the benefits of His care.

The dove David spoke about in Psalm 68 was the army of Israel. While God was at work defeating the enemy, His dove slept safely by the campfires. After the battle, because of His great love for Israel, God adorned her with plunder from the victory.

There are several astounding battles recorded in the Bible, where God went ahead of His people and won the battle before they even stepped out of camp. Before Joshua and the Israelites marched around Jericho the people there were already trembling in fear. (Joshua 2:8-11; 5:1) Before David met the Philistines in battle, God's troops marched out to meet them. (2 Samuel 5:22-25)

When the Arameans laid siege to Samaria, God frightened them off with the sounds of His great army. All that was left for the Samarians to do was gather the plunder. (2 Kings 7:5-7) The angel of the

Lord put to death 185,000 Assyrians with one cuff of His mighty hand when they planned to attack Jerusalem. (2 Kings 19:32-36) The Israelite army never even shot an arrow.

But my favorite story shows King Jehoshaphat's faith in God. The king believed God when He told him his people would not have to fight the battle. So King Jehoshaphat put the choir in front of the army to praise God for His holiness. The enemy fled, not because they were such bad singers, but because God set ambushes on them from every side. In the confusion they turned against each other and slaughtered their own army. And what was left for the Israelites to do when they showed up at the battle field? They worked the next three days collecting plunder! Then they had another praise service. (2 Chronicles 20:15-30)

What battle are you facing this week in your home school? Have you laid it out before God and admitted your helplessness in the face of the enemy? Have you recognized who God is and praised His awesome power? He waits for us, His people, to call on Him, so He can go ahead of us to defeat the power of the enemy. You may have to fight, but then again He may have it all wrapped up before you get there. In any case, put on your armor, praise God, and enjoy the blessings of being His precious dove.

Holy God, your love is so
great and we are thankful!
When everything looks
hopeless and the enemy
looms large, you delight in
showing us your mighty
power. We stand back in
surprise, and awe, and
grateful praise. You are
wonderful! Help me
remember to keep my eyes
on you, Lord, and my ears
attentive to what you would
have me do. I will not fear,
because I know you are
fighting this battle. Amen.

Not Worthy
TO BE COMPARED

I consider that our present sufferings
are not worth comparing
with the glory that will be revealed in us.
Romans 8:18

There are many things in life that people are willing to endure because of the rewards they bring. The pain of physical training brings strength and endurance to win the race. Toiling over words and concepts in school develops a quick mind and knowledge for life. A garden takes hours of sweaty toil to break the sod, plant the seed, pull the weeds, and keep bugs at bay, but the rewards are lush foliage, bright flowers, and satisfying fruits and vegetables.

If we are willing to endure these brief hardships to gain something of worth, certainly we can apply this to whatever spiritual pain we must face as well. Missionaries head purposefully into years of sacrifice, loss, discouragement, and sometimes death to bring the Gospel to people who have never heard of Jesus. Some are never able to see the fruit of their work.

Allen Francis Gardiner saw the need for missionaries and set out to fill it. He headed for South America and was blocked three separate times by government interference and intertribal fighting. On his third try, he recruited six missionaries to join him. He wrote, "I have made up my mind to go back to South America and leave no stone unturned, no effort untried… while God gives me strength, failure will not daunt me." (from *On This Day* by Robert J. Morgan) All seven men died of disease, starvation, and exposure on Picton Island. Gardiner never saw a single person saved for all his efforts, but the South American Missionary Society, which he began, has been sending out missionaries for over 150 years and seen many come to Christ. [6]

Peter Marshall, a Scottish immigrant pastor and chaplain of the United States Senate for two years, refused to let the specter of death frighten him. He served God to his fullest with joy, energy, and humor. His wife, Catherine Marshall, wrote of him in *A Man Called Peter*, "Ever since Peter's own brush with death at the time of his heart attack, there had been an added note of authority in his preaching that went straight to the heart of things." After that experience, Peter saw precious human life only in relation to time and eternity, which is its true perspective."

One day, Peter received a call that a close friend of theirs had died. Peter came into the room where Catherine was. "Gertrude died about ten minutes ago," he said thoughtfully. "I wonder what thrilling experience she's having at this very moment."[7]

The suffering of illness, prejudice, persecution, death—are not worthy to be compared with the wonderful future which awaits us in heaven. Knowing that makes the present more endurable. The prize is worth the effort of the race.

Have you faced persecution because of your faith, because you home school? Then praise God! You will receive glory in heaven beyond compare.

Hold on to that assurance, and remember to pray for those being persecuted today in other countries, enduring torture and death for the sake of our Jesus.

Dear God, it is hard to comprehend how glorious heaven will be—when sin is banished and there are no more tears and heartaches. Please increase my faith so I may willingly endure all that may happen to me in this world. I lift to you all those who are in dark cells today, hungry and cold, hunted down because they bear your Name. Comfort them with visions of their future glory, a glory so resplendant it is not even worth comparing to these present sufferings. Give us understanding, Lord. Amen.

The SKILLED WORKER

Do you see a man skilled in his work?
He will serve before kings;
he will not serve before obscure men.
Proverbs 22:29

*H*ave you ever felt obscure? We work at home behind closed doors, walking the treadmill of lesson plans, school, dishes, laundry, dust, meals, church and sports activities. It seems like no one sees, no one cares. And yet, we know we are not invisible to God, or even to the world around us.

I want to be skilled in my work, not to compete with other home schoolers or the public school, but because I believe in what I'm doing. I place high value on teaching our children how to think, solve problems, and communicate effectively. I want to raise children who know the Gospel and how to share it with others; children who care about people and the world they live in.

As I think about people I know who are good at what they do, I notice they share a few things in common:

1. They use the right tool for the job
2. They mingle with others of their profession, and
3. They use their own style.

My husband, Jeff, is a graphic designer. At first, he worked at a light table with paper, velum and exacto knife. Gradually that changed to a computer. Now, with technology changing so quickly he uses computers, laser printers, photo scanners, FAX and e-mail to keep up with his clients' needs. He is continually having to update his equipment to keep up with the pace of graphic arts today.

We have many tools available to us as home

schoolers. But we don't have to be ruled by the world around us. We must decide what fits into our budget, meets our specific needs, and will provide lasting benefits for us and our children. Whether it's curriculum, manipulatives, computer programs, or books, it's our privilege to choose the best tools for the job.

Almost every profession has conventions and training sessions where people can get together and share ideas, new discoveries and methods, and challenge each other to excellence. Why shouldn't we take advantage of times when we can mingle with other home schoolers to glean ideas, share triumphs and heartaches, and be inspired? Whether it's a convention or a picnic, it's good to know you're not alone. Reading good books and magazines for home schoolers also helps us learn more about our profession.

Then there's the way we go about our work. Every skilled worker has his/her own special style. Some people work quickly and think as they go, others need to plan and move methodically. Some like working outside, while others like being indoors. Some people like working in a quiet corner, others enjoy being with people all day.

We each have our own temperament, energy level, and areas of expertise. Our families operate differently, our children have different needs and learning styles, and we live in a variety of life circum-stances. We can always take in new ideas, but we can't force ourselves into a working style that's not our own. No matter how good it looks at somebody else's house, it will only be a cheap imitation at ours. We must learn to appreciate our strengths and strengthen our weaknesses.

Yes, if we are skilled workers our work will become known, but we don't know how or when. We may not be honored as the teacher of the year at a presidential banquet. Instead, our children will be our trophies. Their children will be inheritors of the work we have done in our home. No, we do not serve in obscurity, we serve before the King of kings.

Dear Lord, I want to be a skilled worker for you, for my children, and for whatever generations may follow before your return. Some days I do feel obscure. Help me see the importance of what I am doing and to get excited about our future prospects. I will serve you, my King, with all my heart, all my mind, all my soul, and all my strength. Amen.

Needing AFFIRMATION

And let the loveliness of our Lord, our God, rest on us,
confirming the work that we do.
Oh, yes. Affirm the work that we do!
Psalm 90:17 (The Message)

The words of that verse wash over me like cool water, soothing and refreshing. To think of the loveliness of the Lord resting on me is an awesome thought! God allows the beauty of His character to settle over us as a way of confirming the work we do.

Do you ever have your doubts about your choice to home school? If your answer is yes then you have probably already prayed a prayer much like this, perhaps many times. We all need affirmation that what we're doing is right and that we're doing a good job of it, but how much more so when our work affects the lives of our children for a lifetime.

The word "confirm" means, "to support or establish the certainty or validity of; verify." Another meaning is, "to make firmer; strengthen." *(American Heritage Dictionary)* So when God confirms our work as parents and home schoolers He gives us support, says that our work is valid. He makes us stronger.

The Greek word, kuroō, is similar but adds the phrase, "to impart authority or influence." *(Vine's Expository Dictionary)* God also imparts His authority to us. We have influence over our children for His good.

Eugene Petersen also uses the word "affirm" in his translation of Psalm 90:17. At first glance this word seems to mean the same thing as "confirm," but there are slight differences. To "affirm" means, "to declare positively or firmly; maintain to be true." *(American Heritage Dictionary)* We need, we desire God's affirmation, for Him to declare with a no-nonsense voice that what we are doing is true and right.

Written words of affirmation mean so much to me when all I can see are clouds of doubt, when I'm sure I'm ruining my children for life by teaching them at home. I find them in God's Word. There are several verses I hold especially dear, because they were His word for me at a particular time for a particular need. Whenever I need confirmation, I can turn to the pages of my journal where I've recorded each verse and what it meant to me at the time. This helps me hold tightly to His promises.

If you have not yet claimed a "mission statement" or theme verse for your school, or for yourself as a teacher, I invite you to ask God to help you find one. As you have your daily quiet time, let the Spirit of God draw you to a particular verse that speaks to you. Write it down along with your response to Him. You can keep these words of confirmation for your own times of questioning, or even as a ready response (and witness) when others question your decision to home school.

Dear God, oh how I need your affirmation!
Sometimes it seems like the whole world
is against our efforts to raise godly
children. Sometimes the battle is within
me and I need your touch to let me know
it's worth it all. I may not receive a raise
or a bonus, but your rewards are of
greater value. I seek to please you, Lord.
In Jesus' Name, Amen.

April

PLANTING FOR A
FUTURE HARVEST

What Kind
OF SMART ARE YOU?

There are different kinds of gifts,
but the same Spirit.
There are different kinds of service,
but the same Lord.
There are different kinds of working,
but the same God works all of them
in all men.

1 Corinthians 12:4-6

In Marlene LeFever's book, *Learning Styles*, she says the way we teach should not ask, "Are you smart?" but, "What kind of smart are you?" She describes four main learning styles, but the way our school and Sunday School classrooms are geared, we cater only to the auditory learner (the one who learns by hearing lectures or verbal instructions). This leaves three fourths of the people in schools and churches frustrated, unmotivated, feeling ignorant because they don't learn the way most teachers teach.[8]

This is information we can really use as home schoolers. (See also Cynthia Tobias', *The Way They Learn*) Every good parent knows no two children are alike. Each one is an individual with a different approach to life and its problems and joys.

My Dad told me when my oldest sister, Kathy, was born, my parents learned how to parent by trial and error. When Linda came along, they thought they'd worked out some of the bugs of this parenting thing, but she didn't respond to the methods they'd used the first time around. "Then," he said, "you were born, and none of what we'd learned so far did us any good."

Of course, he was exaggerating a little. I wasn't that difficult a child and there are some things that never change in the parenting game. But it is true that my two sisters and I are three completely different people and what worked with one didn't always work with another. My parents did a good job of valuing each of us for who we were created to be. They encouraged us to develop our individual talents.

Now I have two girls of my own and two nieces—all very different and wonderful in their own way. Tara loves singing, drama and adventure. Launa loves tools, maps, and playing with friends. Heidi loves books, track, and playing the clarinet. Amy loves playing the fiddle, horses, and books. All these girls are created by God to fill a different niche in the world and fulfill God's purposes. All learn differently and at different rates. Each one is smart in a special way.

Sometimes I forget this, though, and get frustrated with my girls. One is more of an auditory learner like me, so I expect her sister to learn that way too. Not so. I am tempted to think of this child as a slow learner, but when I present information "her" way I'm amazed how well she catches on. This is more time consuming at the moment, but we win in the end because she is more motivated and attentive when I'm attuned to her needs.

The more I read about learning styles, the more I realize each human being is a great treasure. Some are book smart, some are artistically or musically smart, some are number smart, or mechanically smart, or people smart. Our job is to discover what kind of smart they are and help them value themselves and others as unique individuals as they learn and grow.

This is one of the huge advantages we have over public or private schools. No one knows our children like we do. No one else has the time or resources to discover what will best reach each child and stimulate him or her to learn. We can help them discover their value in God's scheme of things.

Dear Lord, help me resist the temptation to label my children, compare them to others, or barrage them with lessons that don't connect with their minds. Help me see them as you see them, fearfully and wonderfully made. They will probably never think like I do, or always absorb information the first time through (I certainly don't). Show me how to get to know them and how to teach them in their own "language." I praise you for making us all smart in special ways. Help me approach every person I meet with this thought in mind. Amen.

Second
CHANCES

A bruised reed he will not break,
and a smoldering wick he will not snuff out.

Isaiah 42:3

*B*en first met Matt when his mom was helping at the local grade school. He apparently received little care at home, but managed to get himself to school everyday, even though he was usually dirty, hungry, and lacked adequate clothing. After much prayer, Ben's parents invited Matt to come live with them. His mother, a drug addict, lost her parental rights soon after.

Matt lived with their family for three years, until Ben was a senior in college. When Ben's family was unable to adopt him, the state placed Matt with another family. One year later, he was dropped off at Childrens Services Division and put through the painful process of being unadopted; his problems had proved too great for a once hopeful family. Matt's presence in their home had torn them apart.

Kids like this abound—hurting, afraid to trust, doubting that love even exists for them. They are the bruised reeds and smoldering wicks of society.

Now grown, Ben is married. He and his wife Teresa have felt God's call to provide a loving environment for boys like Matt, a place where God's love is modeled and held out to them. If only they will take it. Many times they don't.

Ben and Teresa had only been married one year when Matt came to live with them. He was being released from the Detention Home and needed somewhere to live for awhile. Years ago, Matt had looked up to Ben as his big brother, but his experiences since then have made it hard to trust again. A year after coming to live with Ben and Teresa he ran away, his old life pulled at him too strongly. Another year went by and he came back, seeking, questioning, only to run away again, getting in deeper trouble with the law.

Other boys have joined Ben and Teresa's family, and all but one have run from the love held out to them. It was so discouraging they took a break from foster care, but it wasn't long before God began to tug at their hearts again.

In the meantime they learned to depend on God for everything in prayer, and that they are not responsible for the results of their obedience. Only God can heal a bruised reed, or light a smoldering wick. And so, hesitantly, they prayed for God to lead their steps. Ben and Teresa agreed Ben should quit his job to be a full time dad to the boys God brings their way, whose biggest need is to have a father. Now they are foster parents again.

Isaiah 42:3 has been their theme verse. The Servant of God will not break a bruised reed, or snuff out a smoldering wick. God doesn't consider anyone a lost cause. This is what keeps Ben and Teresa from giving up when, humanly, love is impossible.

Doris Sanford, author of many books for children who have experienced deep hurt and tragedy, says much the same thing in her book, *Love Letters: Responding to Children in Pain*. "Lifelong emotional disability does not have to follow early childhood trauma. I believe that all of us—no matter our age or our pain—have been provided the opportunity to grow and to become emotionally and spiritually sturdy… If you have experienced childhood pain, hang in there. Life can be better! What is crucial to our ability to grow and become strong is our response to those circumstances—and the support that surrounds us." [9]

I know a few bruised reeds. Life has been hard on them. They are wounded and bleeding. And I know some smoldering wicks. They try to live for Christ, but the flame just doesn't last. I get tired of holding them up in prayer, because I don't see progress. I get discouraged. But with Jesus, no one is too far gone to be saved.

Perhaps you have a bruised reed or a smoldering wick in your own home, or in your extended family. You've been tempted to give up, saying, "They'll never change. They're right back where they started from." The Messiah came to seek and to save those who are lost. He will encourage any flicker of life, no matter how feeble. The next time that person reaches out to God may begin a whole new way of life for them in Christ, that lasts forever.

Dear God, forgive me for giving up too soon at times. Give me a heart like yours, full of compassion and forgiveness. Help us remember in our school prayer time this week to pray for those who have been battered and bruised by sin. May my attitude toward these people model your attitude to my children. Help us not to grow weary in loving those who don't yet know how to love back. In Jesus' Name, Amen.

Following
AT A DISTANCE

But Peter followed Him at a distance to the
high priest's courtyard.
And he went in and sat with the servants
to see the end.
Matthew 26:58 (NKJV)

The scene at the Garden of Gethsemane had been strange and horrible. First, Jesus had been so sad and full of foreboding. Then when the soldiers came to take Jesus away, He had gone without a fight. When Peter tried to defend Him, he had been rebuked.

Peter was sad and confused and afraid. And yet, he followed. What would happen now?

He followed Jesus and the mob into the courtyard. He knew the danger. He knew he might be taken too. But still, he had to see what was happening to the Lord.

Peter sat with the servants. It must have been humbling to be there in that strange, uncomfortable place, and yet Peter stayed. He stayed to see the end.

Even though Peter eventually denied his Master, his love for him is also evident in the very fact that he was there. He was afraid. He began to run like the others, but instead followed at a safe distance to see what would happen to Jesus. He intended to stay to the end, but when he began to attract attention Peter denied the One to whom he had earlier sworn allegiance.

However, notice the difference between Judas and Peter. When Judas betrayed Jesus he ran. He ran until he could go no further, then ended his own life in despair. Peter vacillated between love and fear. Even when fear won out for the moment, and he denied the One he'd sworn to die for, he couldn't stay away. He wept bitterly, he repented, and he came back to see the end.

There have been times in my life when I've followed at a distance. I'm not where I want to be spiritually. My prayers are dry and hang in the air about me like helium balloons, the Bible offers no fire for my heart, and although I love my Master, I, too, follow at a distance.

Sometimes it is fear that holds me back. The surroundings are unfamiliar to me and I'm not sure where to go. The Lord has gone in a different direction than I was prepared to follow, and I've been rebuked when I thought I was doing right. Sometimes I hesitate out of self-preservation. If I stick too close to Jesus, I'm sure I will be made to suffer and I'm not ready for that.

It's hard to be a leader and teacher when I feel far away from my Source of wisdom and strength. The truth sounds empty in my ears. That's when I need to do what Peter did—weep, repent, and come back to see the hope and victory of the resurrection. Then I will be reinstated like Peter, to serve Jesus His way, the way of the cross.

Are you facing a dry time in your own spiritual life? Keep following, even if it's at a distance. Ask the Lord to show you what barrier has come between you. Allow Him to draw you near.

Dear Lord, I feel such a responsibility to be always up, always spiritual, always full of the joy of the Lord, because these kids look to me to guide them. But sometimes I get bogged down. Suddenly, I'm far away from you and don't know how to get back. Show me the way, Lord. Point out the sin that has separated us. Cleanse me and make me new. I want to follow close to you.

In Jesus' Name, Amen.

Pleasant
WORDS

A wise man's heart guides his mouth,
and his lips promote instruction.
Pleasant words are a honeycomb,
sweet to the soul and healing to the bones.
Proverbs 16:23-24

$\mathcal{D}$o you ever find it hard to be pleasant to your children? When our girls' schoolwork is sloppy, their bickering constant, chores left undone (after numerous reminders), and they have chosen to disobey my instructions, being pleasant does not come automatically to me. Sometimes it doesn't come at all.

Instead, I tend to bear down with criticism, barking orders at the troops, accompanied by steely glares. The funny thing is, when I use these tactics we only drift farther from the goal. The goal is instruction, to teach my children wisdom and self-control.

Solomon said, "a wise man's heart guides his mouth." When my intellect is the guiding force, it reasons, "That action/attitude from said child does not correspond to my instructions. Punish!" When my mind is in control there is no mercy, only facts. To be wise, I must train my mouth to speak from my heart, adding mercy—the honey that makes instruction and discipline palatable.

When I am tender toward my children my words reflect that softness. My love for them takes into account their intentions and feelings. That's when the barriers come down and real instruction begins—with hearing, understanding, and obedience.

Pleasant words are sweet and delicious, and healing in a world where much of what is spoken wounds and tears the spirit. Being pleasant doesn't mean we have to be silly, sappy, sweety-pies, but sincere, loving, and kind, even when the words we must speak are hard ones. Obedience is still required, but not at the sacrifice of love.

Dear Father, thank you for the way you speak to me. You feed my spirit with the honey of your Word. It comforts and heals me. You also challenge, rebuke and discipline me, but without crushing my spirit and destroying my hope. Your words are pleasant, not because I always want to hear what you say, but because they are true. I am assured of your love for me, even when I have been disobedient. Help me to be more like you. Show me better ways of communicating with these children in my care. Give me a wise and understanding heart to guide my words. Amen.

May

SENDING THEM FORTH

Giving
LAVISH PRAISE

Every day I will praise you
and extol your name for ever and ever.
Psalm 145:2

To extol means to praise lavishly. The word lavish conjures up pictures in my mind like a thick brownie with ice cream, covered with chocolate and carmel sauce. Lavish is Beethoven with a full orchestra, plush carpet with an inch thick pad underneath. Lavish is over and above what is necessary, more than enough. So what is lavish praise?

Kathy told me about a gift she had made, a basket lined with floral fabric and a stenciled inset in the front. She had labored long and it had turned out well, but she wanted reassurance. She showed it to her husband to get some praise and what did he say? "That's nice honey."

"That's nice honey? That's all you can say, 'That's nice honey'?" she responded with disappointment.

He looked at the basket again and said, "Oh, that was the man response, wasn't it? You wanted a *woman* response, didn't you?"

She nodded. To her delight he went back to the doorway, put his hand on his hip and minced back into the room. Then he picked up the basket and said, "Oh kid, you made this? Oh, I just don't believe it! Look at that gorgeous material and that CUTE stenciling you did on the side. However did you do it? I just love it, kid!"

Now that's lavish praise. It may not have been totally sincere, but it satisfied a need in her, a reward for what she had done. She laughed and loved every minute of it.

I wonder if God sometimes feels the way

Kathy first did about my praise to Him. "You mean that's it?" He might say. "That's all you're going to say about the world I've created, the miracles I've done, the lives I've changed and the blessings I give you each day. 'That's nice'?"

Maybe I need to exit my prayer closet and come back in again, and with sincere words of admiration for who God is and what He has done in my life, my church, our world, and in all of history give Him some real praise. Instead of a hard, dry crust of bread, I want to give my God a generous, heaped up portion of praise dessert—lavish praise.

David said he would praise God like that every day, that he would extol His name forever and ever. If we truly believe God is God, we will be doing just that, for all eternity. We might as well begin practicing now, privately, in church, and in our school, so King David and the angels won't outdo us when we get to heaven. We will be singing together:

Holy, holy, holy is the Lord God Almighty,
who was, and is, and is to come.
You are worthy, our Lord and God,
to receive glory and honor and power,
for you created all things,
and by your will they were created
and have their being.
Worthy is the Lamb, who was slain,

to receive power and wealth and wisdom and strength
and honor and glory and praise!
To him who sits on the throne and to the Lamb
be praise and honor and glory and power,
for ever and ever!
from Revelation 4,5

Dear God, my Father, you are
indeed worthy of praise. Help
me teach our children the
meaning of lavish praise.
I want to praise you in true
devotion and thankfulness for
all you've done for me.
I cannot grasp the extent of
your love for us. I cannot
fathom your wisdom and the
perfection of your plan for
mankind. But I worship you,
Lord. I will extol you today,
and every day, forever. Amen.

Speaking
OF GOD...

They will speak of the glorious splendor of your majesty,
and I will meditate on your wonderful works.

Psalm 145:5

We sing, "What a Friend We Have in Jesus" and talk about God's blessings and kindness. But I wonder, have I forgotten to teach my children about the majesty of God? Can I comprehend it myself? He is approachable only because of what Jesus has done for us. How often do I stop and contemplate His power and awesome splendor?

Maybe it would be worthwhile to introduce my girls to passages that focus not just on the teachings and stories of Jesus, and the standard children's Bible stories, but also include those verses that describe God, written by those who have seen His glory.

One can't help but imagine the amazing scene which Isaiah 6 describes, *"I saw the Lord seated on a throne, high and exalted, and the train of his robe filled the temple."* He was surrounded by angels saying," *'Holy, holy, holy is the LORD Almighty; the whole earth is full of his glory.' At the sound of their voices the doorposts and thresholds shook and the temple was filled with smoke."*

Then there's Elijah's incredible experience on Horeb, the mountain of God. He was discouraged and afraid. He needed to see God's power as well as His gentleness. *"The LORD said, 'Go out and stand on the mountain in the presence of the LORD, for the LORD is about to pass by.' Then a great and powerful wind tore the mountains apart and shattered the rocks before the LORD, but the LORD was not in the wind. After the wind there was an earthquake, but the LORD was not in the earthquake. After the earthquake came a fire, but the LORD was not in the fire. And after the fire came a gentle whisper."* (1 Kings 19:11-12)

And Daniel had a vision of God the Father: *"thrones were set in place, and the Ancient of Days took his seat.*

His clothing was as white as snow; the hair of his head was white like wool. His throne was flaming with fire, and its wheels were all ablaze. A river of fire was flowing, coming out from before him. Thousands upon thousands attended him; ten thousand times ten thousand stood before him. The court was seated, and the books were opened." (Daniel 7:9-10)

He also saw the Son of God in His glory: *"In my vision at night I looked, and there before me was one like a son of man, coming with the clouds of heaven. He approached the Ancient of Days and was led into his presence. He was given authority, glory and sovereign power; all peoples, nations and men of every language worshiped him. His dominion is an everlasting dominion that will not pass away, and his kingdom is one that will never be destroyed." (Daniel 7:13-14)*

These descriptions are a far cry from the stained glass pictures we have of a weak, pale Christ and the Santa Claus God so many envision today. Our God is good, gentle, and loving, but He is also holy, and majestic in power; our God is a consuming fire.

In C.S. Lewis's *The Lion, The Witch and the Wardrobe*, Lucy asks Mr. and Mrs. Beaver if Aslan is safe. Mrs. Beaver answers, "If there's anyone who can appear before Aslan without their knees knocking, they're either braver than most or else just silly." "Then he isn't safe?" said Lucy. "Safe?" said Mr. Beaver. "Don't you hear what Mrs. Beaver tells you? Who said anything about safe? Course he isn't safe. But he's good. He's the King, I tell you."[10]

I need to spend time focusing on these neglected attributes of God with my children. I plan to

read these passages to my girls and have them draw
what they imagine it was like for Isaiah, Elijah, and
Daniel to see the glory of God. I know what my picture
would look like. I would make it as big as the side of
a house and so bright it would hurt your eyes. Heaven
would be white and gold and silver, and God's robe
would be purple, scarlet, and blue. And I would be on
my face at His feet, in awe of my wonderful God.

God, you are an awesome God.
When I read such passages from
the Scripture I am humbled and
kneel before you in adoration.
Who am I that you would use me?
And yet, you have cleansed me
with fire from your altar, just as
you purified the lips of Isaiah, so
he could speak your words to the
people. When I see you in your
holiness, in your power and glory,
I tremble to draw near. But you
have called me and you are good.
Touch my lips that I might speak
for you. Amen.

Tell
...PROCLAIM!

They will tell of the power of your awesome works,
and I will proclaim your great deeds.
Psalm 145:6

To tell: "1. To give a detailed account of; narrate." Some of my favorite books are told in third person via a narrator—John Steinbeck's *Cannery Row* and *Of Mice and Men*; Jane Austen's *Sense and Sensibility* and *Emma*. Telling a story this way draws the reader into the book. The reader feels like he's watching the events with a friend who knows the characters intimately.

This is one way we can share God with our children, by giving a detailed account of Christian history and taking on the role of the narrator. I would call this the Story style of sharing Christ. We have intimate knowledge of the characters in the Bible because of our own familiarity with the accounts. We can draw our children into the outpouring of God's love by telling them in story form.

Two more definitions of the word "tell" (from the *American Heritage Dictionary*) are: "2. To communicate by speech or writing; express with words. 3. To make known to; notify, inform." These are what I would term the Teaching style of sharing Christ. In this way we impart information about the God whom we serve. Communicating through written and spoken words captures those hungry for knowledge of the living God.

A final definition of the word "tell" is, "4. To make known; reveal." This I would call the Personal style of sharing Christ. When we reveal something to others we show them a deeper part of ourselves. We draw the listener in through his feelings when we tell about personal victories and defeats.

We do these three things every day as home schoolers, whether we officially plan to or not. We narrate God's Word to our students, we communicate the message through teaching, and when we honestly share our struggles and joys, we make the Christian life known to our children in a way that will touch their emotions.

But David also said he would proclaim God's great deeds. Proclaiming requires a going forth to spread the word.

Once again I went to the dictionary for a fuller understanding. Proclaim means: "1. To announce officially and publicly; declare. 2. To indicate unmistakably; make plain. 3. To praise; extol."

To do this we don't have to stand on street corners, or be missionaries. We can proclaim wherever we are. Gayle Erwin, author and speaker on *The Jesus Style*, tells about his experience on an airplane in his book, *That Reminds Me of a Story*. It began when the man seated next to Gayle asked him what he did for a living.

Gayle answered, "I have more fun than anybody. I go all over the world teaching on the Nature of Jesus."

"I'm not a religious man myself," he shot back.

Gayle was able to answer without getting defensive and the discussion continued. Finally Gayle said, "Suppose you are right and I am wrong. I am not rich, but I am having so much fun I can hardly stand it. I harm no one, I eat and sleep well. If you are right, tell me what have I lost?"

"Nothing!" the man answered.

"But if I am right and you refuse to know and serve God, what have you lost?"

His response was quick, "Everything!"

When they got to the gate, Gayle suddenly realized the whole cabin had been listening to their conversation. He gave the CEO his card and invited him to call. When the group exited they were quiet and thoughtful. The Word had been proclaimed.[11]

We can proclaim Christ too, in our own way, causing people to stop and think about their response to Him. Asking questions and giving honest answers in a non-threatening way can open doors for us to proclaim the Good News.

Lord, I have to admit I'm better at telling than proclaiming, but I want to proclaim my faith to the world. I want to make it plain and simple and full of love. Help me this week to tell my children about you. Lead me also to proclaim my love for you everywhere I go, boldly and with great joy. Amen.

Passing
ON THE FAITH

One generation will commend your works to another;
they will tell of your mighty acts.
Psalm 145:4

What does it mean to commend God's works from one generation to another? The *American Heritage Dictionary* says it means: "1. To represent as worthy, qualified, or desirable; recommend. 2. To express approval of; praise. 3. To commit to the care of another; entrust."

How rich is that one word!

When I need a babysitter, I often ask friends who they might recommend. I look for someone who is qualified to do the work. They must do work that is worth the pay. And they must be a desirable person, someone with whom I want my children to spend time.

If Suzanne, who has been recommended to me, turns out to be terrific I will tell her what a good job she is doing. I will praise her to her parents and to my friends and recommend her to my friends. Others will want to have her come to their home as well, because I have recommended Suzanne so highly.

If Suzanne cares about my children, plays with them, watches out for their safety, and gives them her full attention when she is "on the job," I will have no problem entrusting them to her care. I would say she does a commendable job.

This is what we do when we commend God's works to the next generation. If we recommend Him highly, praise Him freely, trust Him fully, our children will want to follow Him and so will many others.

Some of His works and mighty acts are recorded in the Bible, but that is only the beginning. We can find evidence of Him everywhere. Our curriculum daily gives God praise for His creation and power. And we each have stories which reveal God as worthy of our trust. When we verbalize our praise, giving specific details, we show our children reasons for delighting in Him.

When my husband was a little boy his family traveled around the United States and saw Yellowstone, Mount Rushmore and many other spectacular views along the roadside. Jeff grew weary of stopping at every turnout to see the sights. When his mother encouraged him to look at another magnificent scene he said, "Ah, Mom, it's just another one of God's beautiful creations."

His parents laughed, and so did the other people at the lookout, but Jeff's parents didn't stop commending God's works to him. They just kept right on telling him what a wonderful God they served and what mighty things He has done. And now that little boy has grown up to tell a new generation about this God who has done great things in his life.

Our Father, you have done such wonderful things. You created the universe and keep it running perfectly. You've designed our world in detail and you care about each person in it. I praise you for the mighty acts you have performed throughout history—the way you have saved your people, and led us, and enabled us to understand more about this world and your Word. I will recommend you highly to my children because of these things. I will tell them my story—how you saved me and lead me through every difficulty. Amen.

END-OF-THE-YEAR BONUS

Waiting
FOR THE HARVEST

Let us not become weary in doing good,
for at the proper time we will reap a harvest
if we do not give up.
Galatians 6:9

It is August and I'm already tired of my garden. That's not good, because it's just now harvest time for most vegetables. The peas are done, but the corn is starting to come on strong, and the cucumbers are producing well. The lettuce is growing, and the tomatoes are just now beginning to ripen. Everything is delicious and healthy, almost.

The beans are not doing well. The magnificent sunflowers I planted at the back of the garden shaded the bush beans and the slugs trooped into the shady grove. I don't like slugs. I went out with a baggie one morning, put all the slugs I could find in it, added salt, and tied a knot. Sadistic, I know, but satisfying.

I also put out slug bait. But the beans are not recovering well and I've grown weary of caring for them. I don't know if there will be any more beans this year unless I can keep them sprayed and slug-free. I am tired of the work and next week we go on vacation. I may just pull them out before we go.

I didn't give up on my roses, though. This year I've been fighting blackspot and mildew. At one point it was so bad I had to strip the branches of every leaf to get rid of the affected parts. There was nothing left but short, bare branches. I looked with envy at my neighbor's healthy bushes, covered with fragrant roses.

Since then I have faithfully sprayed each bush with fungicide and cut off any affected leaves once a week. It's starting to pay off. There is new growth, green leaves, and this week we've had roses in the house for the first time all summer, and there are more coming. I'm glad I didn't give up.

What does this have to do with home schooling? I imagine there are some of you whose year didn't go exactly as you had planned. Maybe it was your first year, or maybe it was just an awful year full of disasters from within or without. My word to you is don't give up before you see the harvest. Take some time off to rest and plan your attack, but don't give up on the whole idea.

Sometimes we have to prune things back to get rid of areas affected by disease. It looks ugly for awhile, but at the proper time, or in due season, there will be a harvest. At other times, there are pests that come to ravage a once healthy plant. They have to be removed and the damaged plant coddled and protected while it regains strength. That's what we need to do for our children while they're growing and vulnerable to attack.

Maybe I won't pull up those beans after all. Instead, I think I'll make sure they get the water they need while we're gone, put out fresh slug bait, and see how they're doing when we get back. Maybe there will be some fresh beans for supper again soon, if I don't give up.

Dear God, here we are at the end of the school year and I'm evaluating. There are some places I can see progress, but in other areas I'm discouraged. Help me not to give up before the harvest. Grant me wisdom, Lord, to see where the problem lies and what I can do to help my children grow in this area. Help me be patient for the harvest of godliness and not keep digging up the "seeds" to see if they're growing. I know that there can only be a harvest if I am obedient to you. In Jesus' Name, Amen.

Endnotes

A Reason to Sing

1. Patricia Treece, *A Man for Others: Maximilian Kolbe, Saint of Auschwitz, in the words of those who knew him* (New York, Evanston, San Francisco, London: Harper & Row, 1982).

2. Mark Finley and Steven R. Mosley, *Unshakable Faith: How to Stand Fast in the Worst of Times* (Nampa, ID: Pacific Pipeline, 1997).

Energizing Power

3. Amy Carmichael, *Edges of His Ways* (Fort Washington, Pennsylvania: Christian Literature Crusade, 1955), July 8.

Darkness is Passing

4. Mark Finley and Steven R. Mosley, *Unshakable Faith: How to Stand Fast in the Worst of Times* (Nampa, ID: Pacific Press, 1997).

Velvet Covered Steel

5. Pat Holt and Grace Ketterman, M.D., When You Feel Like Screaming (Wheaton, IL: Harold Shaw Publishers,1988).

Not Worthy to be Compared

6. Robert J. Morgan, *On This Day* (Nashville, TN: Thomas Nelson, 1997).

7. Catherine Marshall, *A Man Called Peter* (Charlotte, N.C.: Commission Press, Inc., 1951), p. 243.

What Kind of Smart Are You?

8. Marlene LeFever, *Learning Styles* (Colorado Springs, CO: Cook Communications, 1994).

Second Chances

9. Doris Sanford, designed by Graci Evans, *Love Letters: Responding to Children in Pain* (Sisters, OR: Multnomah Press, 1991).

Speaking of God

10. C.S. Lewis, *The Lion, The Witch and the Wardrobe* (New York: Collier Books, Macmillan Publishing Company 1950, 1970), p. 138.

Tell... Proclaim!

11. Gayle Erwin, *That Reminds Me of a Story* (Cathedral City, CA: Yahshua Publishing, 1997), p. 127.